Every Day
Holy

---

60 Devotions
To Embrace God's Gift of Time

Meredith Barnes

PARACLETE PRESS
BREWSTER, MASSACHUSETTS

2023 First Printing

Every Day Holy: 60 Devotions to Embrace God's Gift of Time

Copyright © 2023 by Meredith Barnes

ISBN 978-1-64060-911-2

Library of Congress Control Number: 2023942393

10 9 8 7 6 5 4 3 2 1

Published by Paraclete Press
Brewster, Massachusetts
www.paracletepress.com

Printed in the United States of America

To

Ben, Campbell, Warren, and Everett,

who I spend the most time with.

Trust the past to God's mercy,
the present to his love, and the future to his providence.

—SAINT AUGUSTINE

Contents

The Power of Time

Waiting on God

Don't Forget the Journey

A Time For...

Introduction

In the hope of eternal life that God, who never lies, promised before the ages began—in due time he revealed his word through the proclamation with which I have been entrusted by the command of God our Savior.
—TITUS 1:2–3

I first started writing this book in the middle of the COVID-19 pandemic. Like many others, I was quarantined at home—with children ages five, three, and one—and there was very little (if any!) space or time for what I wanted. I wanted time to clean without anyone creating a mess immediately after I had straightened up. I wanted quiet moments during which I could immerse myself in contemplative prayer. I quickly realized that somewhere, buried under all the stress and worry of a family forced together in a small space, there was a gift. The gift of time. In the midst of worrying about the loss of time for myself, I appreciated the time we had as a family.

Here's the thing about time: It's everywhere. Time can feel like a gift and a curse. We can't avoid it. We can't get it back. We can't save it. Time finds its way into everything I do. So, with that in mind, I decided to take a deeper look at all that time has to offer, how God uses time, how I use time, and how I could make better choices with my time.

I would be remiss if I didn't mention that on the other side of earthly time is a bigger promise—a much bigger gift—to all of us. Eternity awaits. It has always existed through the presence of God, our Creator without beginning or end, but it also welcomes us when our time here is done. Just as we might have a tenuous relationship with time, we also have a limited understanding of what comes after living on Earth. Titus 1 reminds us that eternity with God has always been the promise.

I avoided sharing my writing for a long time. I was afraid of not being good enough. I worried someone had already written the words I wished to share—and perhaps even did a better job. I let fear slow me down. I let self-doubt waste my time. And this is perhaps something all of us battle—the feeling of not being enough. But when we allow fear to slow us down, it wastes the beautiful gift of time. It took a severe loss of "time to myself" to force me into recognizing the wealth of beauty and opportunity time has to offer. Time is truly a gift of abundance from the Lord.

I hope this book is an encouragement to you. I hope it is a gentle reminder that we are not designed to be at war with hours, weeks, or years. We are designed to be in harmony with time. And by being in harmony with time, we walk in harmony with our Creator. I pray you begin to experience time and God through a different lens and that these words meet you where you are right now. For such a time as this. . . .

In the Beginning

God's Ultimate Idea

In the beginning, God created the heavens and the earth.

The earth was without form and void, and darkness was over the face of

the deep. And the Spirit of God was hovering over the face of the waters.

—*Genesis 1:1–2, ESV*

I f you are like me, the beginning of things is an exciting time. I love the start. The preparation. The blank sheet of paper. The endless opportunities in what lies ahead. The beginning is special because no mistakes have been made yet. But beginnings can become an idol to me. And that idol can paralyze my creativity. An idea is always at the center of the beginning. And sometimes that idea is so perfect in my mind that it starts to seem impossible for reality to meet my expectations.

There are many times I have stalled at the beginning of something for fear of imperfection. I have procrastinated or simply abandoned perfectly good ideas because I wasn't sure of what the product would be. The beginning is the easiest time to give up because I don't actually see it as giving up. If I stop before I start, no one will ever know. To have no one know I had an idea that might not be successful—doesn't that feel safer? The fear of failure and imperfection are a beginner's biggest adversaries.

In Genesis 1 we see the greatest beginning, the beginning of the universe. The beginning of everything. God had the ultimate idea. He thought of you. And you know what is the most empowering part of God's creation story? He knew it would be flawed. He knew there would be mistakes made by humans along the way. Not small, insignificant mistakes—big, giant, brother-killing, flood-inducing, wife-stealing mistakes. Can you imagine starting with an idea, the most perfect idea ever, and knowing it would be flawed? That it would never be free of imperfection? God knew we would mess things up, and yet, that didn't stop him from moving forward.

Now, it's true, God had a plan for our mistakes. And not just any plan. He had Jesus, a Son who would embody human form and give up his life for all our shortcomings. But just because we're absolved by grace does not mean that on this earth, in this time, we are perfect. We're still flawed. We're God's flawed creation. And he made us anyway.

When we're facing a beginning that may feel intimidating—moving to a new city, starting a new job, learning a new hobby—we can take comfort in the creation story that we read in Genesis. God created the world simply because he loves us, just as a parent loves a child, no matter the mistakes or shortcomings. When we shy away from leaning into the beginning that is before us, we stop living into the love that God extends to us through creation. We stop believing that God is using this beginning as one aspect of time to grow and stretch ourselves. When we embrace the beginning and its many offerings, we embrace time. We embrace God's perfect timing.

Questions

1. Are you excited or scared by beginnings? When did you first recognize these emotions?

2. Do you find you jump into something and then abandon it when things go awry? Or do you never start for fear of failure?

3. How does it make you feel to know that God knew we would be imperfect even as he was creating us?

4. What is something you've been putting off starting? Why?

5. What is something you've started and abandoned? Why?

Let There Be Light

Then God said, "Let there be light," and there was light. And God saw that
the light was good, and God separated the light from the darkness.
God called the light Day, and the darkness he called Night.
And there was evening and there was morning, the first day.

—GENESIS 1:3–5

I went to Alaska one year in May when days are long and nights are hard to find. It's amazing how quickly I was disoriented without a more balanced partnership of night and day. No matter how hard I tried to block out the light when it was time to go to sleep, it was impossible to make it feel like bedtime. When I returned home and was welcomed by the sweet relief of night—true darkness—I was given a glimpse of the gift God designed for us.

Our bodies are connected to the sun. Biologically our bodies suppress certain rest and sleep-related hormones in the presence of daylight. When someone is having sleep issues, some doctors will advise their patients to spend ten or more minutes every morning, when they first wake up, sitting in the sun to help reorient their body rhythms. God created our bodies to be in partnership with the cycle of the sun.

God created time on the first day of his big idea. At the very beginning, thinking about you, he created light, separated it from the darkness, and gave all humanity time in the form of day. If I'm being really honest with myself, I think I go through most of my life viewing time as the enemy. It is something to endure, count down, manage, set alarms for, cram in, or even beat. I never have enough time—or it goes too slowly. There's rarely a day when I have a purely pleasant interaction with time. Maybe this is you, too?

What if, instead, we looked at time as God's first gift to us? God created light in the form of day and then paired it with the darkness of night to give us the *gift* of time, balanced for our well-being. We claim to be grateful for the time we have here on earth. But do we truly have a positive relationship with time?

Time is not our enemy. Time is the beginning of our story. Time grounds us and is designed to help us.

Questions

1. Do you see time as something you are working with or against?

2. How can you work toward treating time as a gift?

3. Are you selfish or generous with your time?

4. How might you invite God to participate in your view of time?

The Rhythm of Time

And there was evening and there was morning, the second day.
—GENESIS 1:8

And there was evening and there was morning, the third day.
—GENESIS 1:13

And there was evening and there was morning, the fourth day.
—GENESIS 1:19

And there was evening and there was morning, the fifth day.
—GENESIS 1:23

And there was evening and there was morning, the sixth day.
—GENESIS 1:31

Each day is different. Some people like the adventure a new day brings. Others—me included—desire few surprises. Whether you are a person of routine or someone who seeks out new experiences each day, God understands every detail of who you are and what you prefer.

I'm drawn to routine, habit, schedule, consistency, whatever you want to call it. In my best moments, I call it discipline. In my worst, I call it controlling. As I read through Genesis, I notice that within the first six days of creation one thing stays consistent—there was evening and there was morning. Whether I want to look at the week of creation symbolically or literally, there was a lot happening throughout that first week of life. The world was drastically changing every day. But I see that as much as things were changing, one thing stayed constant: God's plan of time. Even in the unexpected of the beginning, there was a rhythm.

Evening, morning, evening, morning.

We all live within the rhythm of time. Some days we feel we're in sync. Other days we fight the rhythm. We're running late. We can't catch up. We're behind the beat. It's easy to let time overwhelm us. After all, it stops for no one. In the moments when we find ourselves offbeat and behind, we are challenged to slow down, stop, and remember the purpose of time. Time can be viewed as God's ever-present reminder of his consistency and faithfulness.

Evening, morning, evening, morning.

If we begin to recognize the rhythm and consistency of time as one of the most tangible examples of God's presence in our lives, could we also see time as a comfort rather than a struggle?

I like to arrive early for things, and I tend to get anxious when I'm late. Several years ago, I started practicing an activity whenever I perceived I was running late. Rather than give in to my anxiety and attempt to rush, I would fight my instincts and slow down. I would ask myself this question after a few deep breaths: "What is going to happen if I am late?" Most often the answer to that question revealed my pride or the desire to be liked. While we shouldn't be late to things, and I'm not suggesting we throw caution to the wind and disrespect those around us, I'm proposing a new paradigm. In moments of anxious hustling, could we steal a moment to recognize time as one amazing gift from God? Could we refocus and allow ourselves to embrace the gift—a rhythm offered to guide, not oppress—and find peace in his consistency?

Evening, morning, evening, morning.

Questions

1. Do you seek out routine in your day? Why or why not?

2. How do you feel when you are running late? What automatic thoughts might have to change during these times of pressure?

3. How might you see time as a reminder of God's presence?

4. What is one thing you can do when you start to feel behind that could help you embrace time rather than feel frustration or anxiety?

The Framework of Time

*But do not ignore this one fact, beloved, that with the Lord one day is like
a thousand years, and a thousand years are like one day.*

—2 PETER 3:8

W hy did God take seven days to create the universe when he could have done it in the time it takes to snap your fingers? I believe that by taking seven days to create, he established time for those he created in his image. Humans have not proven to exist outside of time. There is no journey without time. There is no story without the passing of time. No suspense, no relief. God knew our human existence needed a framework—a beginning, middle, and end. But make no mistake, God doesn't need time. Second Peter 3:8 is a powerful statement to us of God's supreme power over all things—including time. God is above time, living in eternity.

If I'm being honest, the thought of eternity scares me. When I was young, I would cry at night at the thought of heaven, living with no end, surrounded by angels, and no change in life or circumstances. I don't actually want to live forever, and I'm not eager to die either. Mostly it's because I don't fully understand what comes next in eternity. And things I don't understand can make me uncomfortable. There is no framework to eternity. As humans we live within certain boundaries—time being a big one. Time allows us some certainties such as when it's time to wake up, eat lunch, pick up kids from school, and a whole host of other things. We use earthly cues like the sunset and moonrise to structure our actions.

I think God knew the absence of time would scare some of us. We are attracted to the before and after concepts that time provides us. We gravitate toward the stories that are firmly supported by time. We value the time stamps in our lives—birthdays, graduation, retirement, anniversaries—that mentally move us through change and transition. Our human hearts and minds need to visibly mark off time and have a sense of forward momentum in our lives.

When we might be overwhelmed by the thought of eternity or what existing outside of time might feel like, we can remember that God is the creator of all things. God is the creator of the earth, the sun, the plants that shade us, the water that quenches our thirst, and all of time. God knew that by establishing time, he was providing for us. And just as he provides these things for our human condition, he will also perfectly provide for us in eternity. Take comfort in the promise that God knows and will supply for all our needs—today, tomorrow, and forever.

Questions

1. Why do you think God created time?

2. Is the idea of eternity overwhelming or comforting?

3. In 2 Peter 3:8 we are reminded that God is not constrained by time. God knows more than the present moment; he knows every detail of each human life. How does this knowledge impact your outlook on life?

4. Name some ways that you have seen God provide for you.

Every Day Holy

This is the day that the LORD has made;

let us rejoice and be glad in it.

—PSALM 118:24

The other day I had the car radio turned to praise and worship music and my son asked me, "Mom, why are we listening to church music? It's not Sunday." I wasn't sure how to answer at first. It was clear he had equated Christian music with Sunday mornings, which I didn't mind. But it seemed he thought that it was *only* for Sunday mornings, which I didn't like.

I explained to him that yes, we worship God on Sunday mornings but we are also blessed when we worship him throughout the week. Even as I shared these words, I recognized that my son wasn't the only one who mistakenly put the Trinity in a Sunday box. Isn't that what many of us do? We designate one day of the week as holy, leaving the other six days to whatever may demand our time and attention. Maybe we even consider Sunday morning worship as something to check off our "good Christian" list that we've created in our minds. But God doesn't just want our attention and time on Sundays. Obviously he wants our voices singing his praises and our hearts softened toward his will every day of the week. God made every day holy.

I like to think of it this way: God is the creator of time, therefore all of time is ordained under his authority and is worthy to be considered holy. What this means is our every action throughout each day has the opportunity to be a holy action. The ordinary can become holy simply by inviting God into the moment.

When I was growing up, my parents would look for ways to help my brother and me prepare throughout the week for the joy to come at church on Sunday. One way they did this was through a practice called "making Sunday special." On Saturday evenings we would gather for homemade liturgies and celebration, preparing our hearts for Sunday but also relishing in the holiness of the current day and time. My parents honored the Sabbath but also reminded us that every day was an opportunity to draw closer to God through our thoughts, words, attitudes, and activities.

There may be seasons in life when worshiping God becomes a "Sunday only" activity, but I pray we don't fall into a rut and limit our big, gracious God. Holy opportunities exist every day and all the time, just waiting for our recognition.

This is the day the Lord has made! Whether it's Tuesday, Friday, or Sunday, each day is a God-sanctioned moment. Not only that, within this day we are called to rejoice and be glad.

Questions

1. In what ways have you set aside Sunday as different from other days of the week?

2. If every day has the opportunity to be holy, how does that change your actions today?

3. How do you rejoice in each day?

4. How can you prepare throughout your week for the worship to come on Sunday?

Jesus Is the Beginning

Jesus said to them, "Very truly, I tell you, before Abraham was, I am."

—JOHN 8:58

on't mess up. Don't mess up. Don't mess up. For a long time, this was the mantra unknowingly playing in my head. I also thought, *I've got to be a good person. I've got to do it all right. I can't mess up.* "Mess up" has meant a lot of different things to me. Sometimes it has stood for sin. Sometimes it has stood for ambiguous life decisions that didn't follow a clear path. The problem is, of course, I mess up. I sin. I make bad choices. I make the wrong choices. For some of you this may seem like no big deal. We all mess up; it's fine. But in the past, I've had a really tough time understanding grace.

"Jesus died on the cross for your sins." I've heard this a lot during my lifetime. And instead of hearing those words transpire into amazing grace, I heard, *Jesus died for you, so you'd better not mess up. You'd better be the best version of yourself. After all, you know Jesus, so you should let that be enough to make you a near-perfect person. Now that you know him? You can't mess up.* Anyone else wrestle with these ideas?

In light of this thought pattern, my routine was: Be a good person, try not to mess up, mess up, feel really bad, speak poorly to myself, ask for forgiveness, beat myself up some more, and try not to mess up again. This loop created a strange relationship between me and Jesus; he was the guy I was always trying to impress.

Then, one day I looked at the timeline and realized Jesus died a long time ago. Obvious, right? But here's the thing. I wasn't always looking at it that way. The fear pattern of messing up I just described centered around an Old Testament way of thinking. I was trying so hard to stay within the lines that I was missing out on a relationship with Jesus. I was offering my guilt in the same way the Jews of the Old Testament had offered up sacrifices for their mistakes.

In John 8, I discovered that Jesus has been around longer than anyone understood at the time. Jesus was at the beginning of time just waiting for his human arrival. Even during Creation, Jesus knew we would mess up thousands of years later. Jesus' sacrifice on the cross occurred before we were born, before we could sin. He came to Earth as a Savior because he knew we couldn't be perfect. When I figured this out, it changed my relationship with my mistakes and with Jesus. I no longer walk around worrying about messing up. I live my life knowing I am fully and unconditionally loved—so loved that God, knowing my sins before I even existed, sent his Son as a sacrifice. God did this to have a relationship with me. That was the plan all along. What freedom!

Questions

1. Are you worried about messing up? What keeps you from having a full relationship with God?

2. How does the fear of messing up affect your relationship with Jesus?

3. What is your natural reaction when you make a mistake?

4. Jesus said, "Before Abraham was, I am." What does that mean to you? Why do you think Jesus shared this?

God Rests
on the Seventh Day

Thus the heavens and the earth were finished, and all the host of them.
And on the seventh day God finished his work that he had done, and he
rested on the seventh day from all his work that he had done. So God
blessed the seventh day and made it holy, because on it God rested from all
his work that he had done in creation.

—GENESIS 2:1–3, ESV

I don't know about you, but this passage feels a little repetitive to me. We get it: God rested. Why does it have to be repeated, using almost exactly the same words each time? Then I think about talking to my children. There are times when what I am saying to them is really interesting, like what's for dessert. They are dialed in to every word I speak when I'm delivering good news. Then there are times when I'm instructing them: *Make your bed. Brush your teeth. Don't hit your brother.* It seems to me that those are the times I am the most repetitive.

Do you ever tune out the Bible? Do you stop listening to God? I do. I tune out the familiar. I tune out the unpleasant. Sometimes I refuse to listen for no good reason at all. God knows this about his children. God knew this about humans before we were even formed.

Sometimes when my kids tune me out, I actually let it slide. I often conduct a risk-reward analysis as I am parenting throughout the day. Sometimes I don't want the fight. Sometimes I back down from the tune-out. In this passage, God is not backing down. What he's doing is important, and he's demanding the reader pay attention, even if it's just to snap us out of a Bible-reading daze to say, *Why did I just read the same sentence multiple times?* Here's why.

Rest is important. There is physical rest, and there is mental rest. Both are important but they demand very different things. In today's world it seems I always have something to do. The house is never clean enough, there is always one more load of laundry, there are appointments to make and keep, the list goes on and on. My mind is scrolling all day. I have a hard time shutting off my to-do list mentality. I struggle sitting next to a pile of anything—clothes, books, toys, clutter. I am driven by compulsivity to keep an organized, well-run household. The problem is, it's hard to turn off. I need God to tell me ten times that it's time to rest. I need permission.

Rest is a hard sell. There's always the pressure to do more, be more, make more. Even as we read Genesis 1, it's easy to pay attention. God is creating! This is where the action is. This is momentum. This is the journey. Then we get to Genesis 2, and he rests. I don't think God was tired. I don't think God actually needs rest, but he makes time for it. And he tells us about it three times in a row. He does all this for us. He sets aside his actions, giving us permission to stop. God rests, and we can, too.

Questions

1. When do you tend to stop listening to God or "zone out" from the Bible?

2. What are some ways you can bring more attention to what God might be saying to you?

3. Are you drawn to rest or to work?

4. What does rest mean for you? How can you improve habitually creating time for rest?

The Alpha and Omega

Then he said to me, "It is done! I am the Alpha and the Omega,
the Beginning and the End. To the thirsty I will give water as a gift from
the spring of the water of life. Those who conquer will inherit these things,
and I will be their God, and they will be my children."

—REVELATION 21:6–7

When Jesus died on the cross he stated, "It is finished": confirmation that he fulfilled God's plan and paid the necessary sacrifice to put us in right relationship with God. Though we might suffer during our time on Earth, in eternity we will live with God, who reigns over evil and triumphs over death. The hard truth is that while Jesus defeated Satan, we will face pain, failure, doubt, loneliness, and a whole host of other problems. Some days we might wake up asking ourselves, "What's the point?" or plead with our Savior, "Please, Jesus, come back soon!"

Human time compared to God's eternity exposes the very real thought that time holds little power over God's faithful followers. From this perspective, we might start to check out and disregard activities or opportunities to participate in the world. We can oversimplify the presence of time along with God's desire to continue ministering, loving, and sharing his gospel. But we must fight against diminishing time's significance and God's intentionality. There is purpose in our time on Earth.

In Revelation we see Jesus recalling his final words of his earthly life, "It is done!" But keep in mind, Revelation is the apostle John's vision of a future promise. It is a revelation of what it will be like when

Jesus returns. This reference, "It is finished!" might be referencing time as humans understand it. In this passage, Jesus goes on to say he is the Alpha and the Omega, the beginning and end. He invites believers into his care, stating he will quench any thirst and take care of us as his own children. We will inherit eternity.

Does time pale in the face of the eternal presence of God and the eternal offering he extends to us? Yes. But that doesn't mean our time here is meaningless. We must hold time with the understanding of just how finite and precious it is. What we do with our time matters. It matters to the one who states *It is finished* yet allows time to continue. It matters as we choose to use our time to learn from and study the One who gifted us this glorious life. Time is but a sliver in the eternal plan. Thanks be that on the other side of time—in eternity—we will experience pure joy and the full radiance of a triune God.

Questions

1. Why do you think Jesus uses the language of beginning and end in Revelation 21?

2. In what ways do you treat time as if it doesn't matter?

3. What would you say to someone who has faced a large portion of suffering or heartache in their time here on earth?

4. God has always been and he will never end—how does this make you feel?

The Promise
of a Fresh Start

Therefore we were buried with him by baptism into death, so that,

just as Christ was raised from the dead by the glory of the Father,

so we also might walk in newness of life.

—Romans 6:4

*T*here is something special about the first page in a new
notebook. Crisp, white sheets, just waiting to be written on
for the first time. The possibilities seem endless. The open
pages offer a welcome fresh start. I also seem to assign this concept
of a fresh start to specific times, mornings, months, years and . . .
Mondays. Raise your hand if you've ever planned to start something
on a Monday. Now keep your hand up if you've fallen off the wagon
before Tuesday has come around.

In the New Testament God is offering us a fresh start. Clearly,
we humans are desperate for a better way, a new covenant. Jesus
the rescuer, savior, giver of new life, enters God's eternal love story.
Crucified, buried, resurrected, and ascended. At the beginning of
Jesus' ministry, he's baptized by his cousin John. *Baptism.* In the New
Testament baptism is a sign of accepting Christ into your life, and it
symbolizes regeneration.

I've been baptized twice. Growing up in the Episcopal church, I
was baptized as an infant. Later in life I became involved in a church
that requested I be baptized as an adult in order to lead a Bible study.
So, I did it. Leading up to my second baptism I felt sort of silly. I've
been a Christian my entire life, and while some seasons have been

better than others, I've never doubted God, Jesus, or the Holy Spirit's working in my life. On the day of my second baptism, I showed up at Lake Michigan at sunrise with a large group from my church. Friends of mine came to support me. I walked into the water fulfilling an obligation, and I walked out with a new beginning. I'm not suggesting baptism every few years of life, but it's worth stating it's never too late for a fresh start or even a simple action to signify renewal and recharge your enthusiasm. The truth for us Christians is we are offered a fresh start every minute of every day through the grace of Jesus. We don't have to buy a new notebook with blank pages every time we mess up or fall short of perfection. Instead, Jesus washes the pages of our life clean simply because we have invited him into our lives.

Change is in your power to create at any time, any place. Maybe your personality is well-suited for starting anew. Or maybe you are a person who is overwhelmed by the list you have created for yourself—the things you have told yourself you can do better. Start small. Check one thing off your list at a time. Give yourself grace to miss an opportunity without it meaning you will not take another opportunity when it arises. We are imperfect creatures working toward a perfect goal that will never be realized here on Earth. But don't let that stop you from trying. Let this be the time for progress, no matter when you start.

Questions

1. What area of your life might need a fresh start?

2. Do you tend to assign fresh starts to a certain time of the day, week, or month? Why do you think you have connected fresh starts to this time frame?

3. How does it make you feel to know that Jesus offers you a fresh start through his sacrificial grace every minute of every day?

4. Have you been baptized? If so, how old were you? What does baptism mean to you?

Time and Anxiety

In a Hurry

Desire without knowledge is not good,
and one who moves too hurriedly misses the way.

—PROVERBS 19:2

Anyone else out there in a hurry? Patience is not naturally one of my strengths, though I continue to work on it. Over the years, I've learned that nothing is made better by hurrying. Slowing down has allowed the sweet moments of my life to reveal themselves—moments I might have otherwise missed. Hurrying seems to be the currency of the day; some people like to justify their hurry by calling it multitasking or "how I'm wired." Many of us are caught up in hurrying from one appointment to the next. We hurry to "fit it all in." Sometimes we hurry and we don't even know why. Or the hurry is to create a false sense of purpose and self-worth.

Proverbs 19 is a helpful warning to those of us who find ourselves hurrying. It gives us two cautions: 1. Desire can be a dangerous influence if we don't slow down long enough to understand the root of our desire, and 2. When we hurry, we can easily end up on the wrong path. It's important to note how desire without knowledge could affect our hurrying. Desire in and of itself is not a bad thing; however, it is when we allow our desires to rule us. If we spend little time understanding our desires, we can get into trouble—often hurrying toward unmerited wants. Many of our desires are based on reaching a perceived finish line. We are hurrying to reach the end, to receive the feeling of accomplishment that we believe is waiting. But when we hurry through the task to reach the end, we often find that the feeling we thought would be waiting for us is a facade.

Sometimes hurrying takes us on the wrong path. We become so focused on reaching the destination that we don't evaluate our trajectory. When we hurry, we make less room for God's direction and rely too heavily on our own direction.

What if we stopped worrying about where we would end up? What if we stopped focusing on our self-constructed happy ending? What if, instead of controlling and rushing to our own planned destination, we simply rested and enjoyed the Holy Spirit's movement and direction?

Many of us are quick to create a list, make the plan, and get to checking off every line item. Sometimes our urge to reach the end causes us to miss the beauty, rush past relationships, and skip the here and now. There's nothing wrong with looking forward or making a plan, but when the horizon becomes more important than the ground beneath our feet or the people venturing with us, we're missing the best part. Time to take a deep breath and re-evaluate.

Questions

1. What pressure do you feel when you are in a hurry?

2. What have you missed by being in a hurry?

3. How can you enjoy the journey as much as the destination?

4. Where might you have "desire without knowledge" in your life? How could slowing down help you gain knowledge?

5. Has hurrying ever taken you on the wrong path? What happened?

The First

For surely I know the plans I have for you, says the LORD,

plans for your welfare and not for harm, to give you a future with hope.

Then when you call upon me and come and pray to me, I will hear you.

When you search for me, you will find me; if you seek me with all your

heart, I will let you find me, says the LORD, and I will restore your fortunes

and gather you from all the nations and all the places where I have

driven you, says the LORD, and I will bring you back to the place from

which I sent you into exile.

—JEREMIAH 29:11–14

can't tell you how many times I've worried about being the first to an idea or a dream. Is an idea even good if it has already been done? The thought that I might work hard to accomplish something, and then discover someone else has done it before me, stops me in my tracks. There have been moments when I've stopped myself from writing this book for fear of it already having been done. What if I'm just one of many? These are relevant fears in a time when everything seems to have been done and actions are publicly critiqued on social media. It's hard to get in at the beginning of a genuinely new idea. We're a society of saturated ideas and countless opinions. So, should we stop creating? Should the probability of being one of many stop any of us from moving forward? I hope not.

In the New Testament, Jesus explains that the first will be last. He lovingly reminds his disciples, and us, that our goal shouldn't be focused on being the first. The amazing thing about the grace Jesus offers is that the positions of first and last have been turned on their heads. From a heavenly perspective they no longer hold significance. When we continue to attempt to reorient our worth and actions to the truth of God's love for us, we understand that being the first to the good idea or the promotion at work neither increases nor decreases God's plan for our lives. When we release the pressure to be the first, we can pursue the things we love and the things that bring us joy without the pressure of accolades.

The encouragement we receive from the words relayed by Jeremiah isn't the promise of welfare. It's better! It's the promise of relationship with God. He doesn't care if we're the first person to the big idea. That has no bearing on his love for us. His plan for all of us is a relationship with him. Every choice we make is either bringing us closer to or further from that relationship. And once we put this eternal truth into perspective, the worry about being first starts to dissipate. We simply need to seek the Lord with all our hearts.

Questions

1. What do you worry about being the first at? How has this affected your actions?

2. Have you stopped pursuing any good ideas because of this?

3. What plans cause you to be excited about God's future for your life?

4. How can freedom in relationship with God give you permission to pursue an idea and stop worrying about the outcome?

It Isn't Too Late

And immediately something like scales fell from his eyes, and his sight was restored. Then he got up and was baptized.

—ACTS 9:18

When I graduated from college with a degree in theology, I had no clue what I was supposed to do next. I had no plan for my future. My first jobs out of college were in the advertising and sales department for the Anaheim Angels and costuming for an independent movie as well as several plays. It was during a job interview that one of the hiring managers encouraged me to decipher what I really wanted for my future.

I remember thinking I wanted to pursue medicine but kept telling myself it was too late. I was too old, and it would take too long to follow that dream. I was in my mid-twenties, which now seems young to me. But as I was contemplating my next life step and watching friends establish themselves in the world, I felt overwhelmed at returning to years of schooling. It felt like a step back rather than a step forward. Nearly one year later, I started applying to schools with the hope of becoming a physician assistant (PA). And when I started graduate school, I was neither the youngest nor the oldest student in the program. There were other people who had also decided it wasn't too late.

In the book of Acts, Saul, who after his conversion became Paul, hated Jesus and everyone who was on Team Jesus. It was Saul's life goal to hunt down, persecute, and kill people who chose to embrace Jesus' message. I love the story in Acts 9 because not only does

Paul have a complete turnaround with his life's purpose, but also it shows us we can change our minds, too. I doubt Paul was pondering whether he should become a disciple. But when the time came and Jesus confronted Paul, his life was transformed. He took a new name and presented himself to the world as a zealous follower of Christ.

Paul didn't have to go public with his new faith. He could have met Jesus, had his conversion experience, and quietly slinked away, ashamed of the persecution he had been instigating. But he didn't. Paul decided it wasn't too late. He was so transformed by his love for Christ that he risked scorn, embarrassment, alienation, and rejection. It wasn't too late.

I became a PA in the fall of 2008, but that wasn't the end of my journey. In 2020, I stepped out in faith again to become a writer. I tell you this to say: I'm still not done. I still wrestle with the question, "Is it too late?" Maybe you do too. Quiet the worry. Shush the conditions you put on yourself. Let God do his mighty work and resolve to change when the Holy Spirit moves you.

Questions

1. Have you ever felt that it was too late for something? How do you feel about that circumstance now?

2. What is one thing God is calling you to accomplish or explore this year?

3. What would you have done if you were Paul? How has knowing Jesus transformed your life?

4. Recall a time when the Holy Spirit took the scales from your eyes and allowed you to have a new hope or perspective.

The Future Becomes Known

With a freewill offering I will sacrifice to you; I will give thanks to your

name, O LORD, for it is good. For he has delivered me from every trouble,

and my eye has looked in triumph on my enemies.

—PSALM 54:6–7

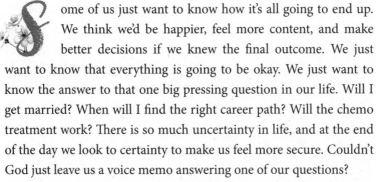 ome of us just want to know how it's all going to end up. We think we'd be happier, feel more content, and make better decisions if we knew the final outcome. We just want to know that everything is going to be okay. We just want to know the answer to that one big pressing question in our life. Will I get married? When will I find the right career path? Will the chemo treatment work? There is so much uncertainty in life, and at the end of the day we look to certainty to make us feel more secure. Couldn't God just leave us a voice memo answering one of our questions?

Deep down we know life is not about certainty. But many days it feels like certainty would equate to happiness. And we try so hard to find secure footholds along the way. What if I said you *can* know the future? There is a way to know it will all be okay. Psalm 54 is our first glimpse; this psalm is one David wrote after he was betrayed by people he had trusted. David was hiding from King Saul, who wanted to kill him and anyone David was with. This should be very stressful for David. Being hunted down in a cave and having your life threatened by a king . . . all of this seems like it would be pretty scary. I'm sure there were big questions swirling around David's mind. It's easy to think David would lament his current circumstance, but when we read verses 6 and 7, we see a different posture from David. He is giving thanks to God. David recalls the many times God has delivered him from trouble. In truth, these words don't sound like someone fearing for his life. I've often wondered, *How can David rejoice in this situation? He doesn't know the future . . . or does he?*

David knows God has protected him in the past. David knows God has brought him to this moment for a purpose. David trusted God in the past, and this allows him to trust God in the present circumstances and even into the future. With God, David's unknown future becomes known. Nothing is a surprise to God; he knows every detail of today and tomorrow. He knew what David needed, and he knows what you need. Unfortunately, this doesn't mean we will have an itemized list of what to expect on the road ahead. We won't know the answers to many of our big questions. But because we know God, who sent down his Son to die for our sins, we have assurance in our eternal future.

When things feel scary and uneasy, remember David and the words he wrote even as he was betrayed into the hands of his enemy. Give thanks in the face of an unknown future because a known Savior has delivered you from every trouble.

Questions

1. What are a few big questions you wish God would answer about the future?

2. How can you take comfort in the certainty God offers in the face of so much uncertainty in the world?

3. Think of a time you felt attacked or overwhelmed but God showed up in your time of need. How did it feel to be caught up in his goodness?

4. How can you maintain a spirit of gratitude and thanksgiving to God throughout each week?

5. Write down a list of the ways God has delivered you or provided for you in the past. Use this list to remind yourself of a known love and salvation from God when the future feels scary and uncertain.

Embrace the Mess

Do not be anxious about anything, but in everything by prayer and

supplication with thanksgiving let your requests be made known to God.

And the peace of God, which surpasses all understanding, will guard your

hearts and your minds in Christ Jesus.

—PHILIPPIANS 4:6–7

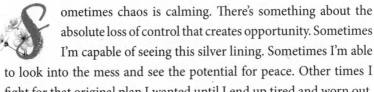 ometimes chaos is calming. There's something about the absolute loss of control that creates opportunity. Sometimes I'm capable of seeing this silver lining. Sometimes I'm able to look into the mess and see the potential for peace. Other times I fight for that original plan I wanted until I end up tired and worn out. Every interaction we have in our day is an opportunity for refinement. Roommates, teachers, bosses, co-workers, spouses, children, even strangers are God's instruments placed in our lives to offer small glimpses of ways we can grow toward him.

Here's what the people in my life have taught me: Life is messy. There are conflicting schedules, differing opinions, and unplanned occurrences that happen all the time. God has taught me that my job is not to resist the mess. My job is not to clean up the mess. My job is to embrace the mess. The mess isn't here to make me anxious. The mess is here to turn me toward Jesus. The mess is here to remind me I need divine help beyond my own capabilities. The passage above doesn't say, "Don't be anxious, and, by the way, figure out the solution to all your problems and never complain." Philippians 4 tells every reader where to look when bogged down by the mess: turn to God. And in doing so we show a willingness to trust God over self. When

I accept my limitations, and therefore the mess, I position myself to accept peace, even in the midst of chaos.

What are ways to embrace the mess and invite God into the daily chaos of your life? It might be giving yourself grace when you don't get an original to-do list done. It might be altering your goals toward the direction God is pointing you. It could be putting another person's needs ahead of your own to serve them.

When we surrender to the messiness of life, we surrender to God's sovereignty. Consider turning to God in prayerful surrender the next time you feel overwhelmed by the chaos surrounding you. Invite the Holy Spirit to come near. Ask for his perfect peace to surpass your will and take time to release how you think things should look, and then watch to see how he answers your prayer.

Questions

1. How do messes make you feel? What types of chaos impact your life?

2. What automatic reactions do you have in times of stress or anxiety?

3. What encouragement do you find in the words of Philippians 4?

4. When was a time that you turned to God in the face of feeling overwhelmed? How did God comfort you?

5. What is one practical way you can attempt to embrace the mess?

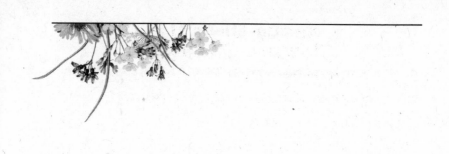

Jesus Calls Us Toward Change

Jesus, looking at him, loved him and said, "You lack one thing; go, sell
what you own, and give the money to the poor, and you will have treasure
in heaven; then come, follow me." When he heard this, he was shocked and
went away grieving, for he had many possessions.

—MARK 10:21–22

Some of you would have no difficulty in selling all your possessions and following Jesus. I'm not that person. When Jesus says leave your family, skip burying your parents, and follow me, I'm not all in. I'm tentative. I'm fearful. As much as I want to follow Jesus and seek a closer relationship with him daily, I can't see him, smell him, touch him—and I really like my family (most days). It's hard to let go. It's hard to commit to upending my life for something I can't see. But then I wonder, if the physical Jesus actually lived next door and asked me to do these things, would it be any easier?

What are some common obstacles you face in following Jesus today? Comfort in how things are now? The unknown of what it will be like if you change? Selfishness? Not trusting God to "go easy" on you?

When we look at Mark 10, we recognize that this young man who stands in front of the physical Jesus is facing an overwhelming change. It's not only a change in physically giving up the comfort of his current life, but also a change in his status within the community around him. It's a significant, life-altering change. Even tiny changes can be hard. The man in Mark 10 was trapped within the constructs of human time. He could not grasp the abundant, eternal promise Jesus was offering him, so Jesus' words caused him to bristle. Jesus was promising this man the eternal gift of a perfect relationship with the Father, Son, and Holy Spirit.

When we consider changes in our lives today it may seem that Jesus isn't asking us to make the same choice he asked of the man in Mark 10. It's easy to think that many of the changes we face in our daily life have no eternal consequences. When we think this way, we diminish the power of Jesus and the Holy Spirit. Everything we do, every minute spent on this earth, has the power to draw us closer to or further from Jesus and an eternal future with him. When we allow comfort in what we know to be more powerful in our lives than the hope of what God has in store for us, we act just as the man in Mark 10 did.

What if you accepted the change God is calling you toward today? Would you act differently? Would you try more "eternal" thinking and put off "earthly" thinking? Give it a try. Walk in obedience toward God today.

Questions

1. Do you find it easier to make a big change for yourself or for Jesus? Explain your answer.

2. What change is God calling you toward that you might be avoiding? Why do you feel uncomfortable making the change?

3. What is one way you can step into God's will for your life?

4. How do you relate to the man in Mark 10?

5. What peace and assurance do you find in knowing Jesus wants the best for you?

When the Plan Changes

The human mind plans the way, but the LORD directs the steps.

—PROVERBS 16:9

'm really good at moping. My brooding is usually centered around a plan changing without my input or permission. And then, after sufficient time of making sure my displeasure has been well documented and everyone around me knows I'm not happy with what's happening, I find a way to get on board. I almost always come around. I almost always recognize my sulking has not stopped the change from occurring or yielded a different outcome. Yet, time after time, I drag my feet in the face of change.

For a long time, I justified my behavior. I explained to others that this was my process. This was how I was able to embrace change and get on board. But the truth is, my process stinks. It usually makes me look ridiculous, and it causes strife with those around me. I'm not suggesting I can't grieve, but I am suggesting I do it with class and grace. The truth is, I've wasted a lot of time being upset about plans changing. Maybe you can relate? Or you know someone who acts like me when the unexpected happens?

My husband and I visited San Francisco several years ago. When we started planning our trip, my one request was that we explore the Redwoods. On the day we planned to venture to Big Basin Redwoods State Park, we rented a car, drove for over an hour, and arrived—only to find out we needed reservations to park and explore the area. I wasn't happy. My moping mood kicked in.

Here's what resulted from our change in plans: We got creative. We decided to go to Golden Gate Park. It wasn't on our list of sights to visit, and we probably wouldn't have gone had we not had the entire morning free with a rental car. We were completely "off schedule" from what I had planned. In the midst of our change, I remembered my favorite part of vacationing with Ben—we adventure well together. I came around a lot faster and was happier for it.

But the truth remains: I am good at acknowledging the *conceptual* need for the unexpected, but so bad at embracing the *actual* unexpected. Over the years I've started asking myself these questions when an unexpected change in plans occurs, to help me gain perspective: What is really bothering me about this change? Am I able to share this with someone I trust (my spouse or a good friend) without dumping on them or fighting with them? Can this lead to a constructive conversation? And most importantly: Am I trusting God and his plan in the midst of unforeseen change?

Proverbs 16:9 reminds us that, as Christians, we are under God's direction. In truth, this should come as a relief. We are not in charge of every detail. But some of us are holding on so tightly to our own plan that we miss God's plan for our time. We continue to resist his control and plan, leading us to miss out on using all our time to the fullest. When we are able to be rooted in the belief that God is establishing our steps, we loosen our grip on the plans we have made. We accept that the plans will change. Our plans for our time within this world are transient. Let us see them as just that and rest in the eternal plan, the one that will never change.

Questions

1. How do you react to a change in plans?

2. What is one way you can practically embrace unwanted changes in your path?

3. Name a situation when you spent too much time having a bad attitude. How could you have handled things differently?

4. How can you use your eternal salvation to combat the anxiety that comes with change?

The Pursuit of Busy

But Martha was distracted by her many tasks, so she came to him and asked, "Lord, do you not care that my sister has left me to do all the work by myself? Tell her, then, to help me." But the Lord answered her, "Martha, Martha, you are worried and distracted by many things, but few things are needed—indeed only one. Mary has chosen the better part, which will not be taken away from her."

—LUKE 10:40–42

'm just so busy. How am I going to get it all done? There aren't enough hours in the day! All these things run through my head on a regular basis. Perhaps some version of these thoughts run through your mind as well. Most of us have regular routines or schedules that we are constantly trying to keep up with, and it isn't until there is some sort of break in the regular activities—a sudden illness or a vacation—that we see just how busy we are and the toll it's taking on our system. There are many things in life that we have little choice about accepting. Sometimes we are busy and feel we have no control over the matter. But what often happens when we step away from the routine of our lives for a stretch of time is that we see glimpses of ways we have made busyness a choice.

When I read this passage from Luke, it takes me a minute to not be slightly annoyed by Jesus. After all, Martha is hard at work, serving those around her. She is getting things done in the kitchen. She sees a need, and she is filling it. Martha is my kind of gal. I am Martha. I also understand Martha's frustration at Mary's getting Jesus' undivided attention. What is this injustice? I want the credit! I want recognition for my busyness.

Jesus doesn't see it that way. He cuts Martha to the core, and us too. He sees our tendency to busy ourselves, and he tells us to stop. The busyness is a distraction from Jesus. It prohibits us from being present in any given moment and invites anxiety into our day. There is something to be learned from Mary in Luke 10. Mary sees Jesus and the time she has with him as important. She resists the call to perform in front of him and instead sits at his feet, relishing the time she has in his presence.

It can be hard to discern when we are pursuing busyness. As we attempt to release the distractions of filling our time, one simple step is to acknowledge the gift of time. To ask ourselves if we are filling our schedule to boost our activity (and maybe our feeling of importance), to escape quiet moments in our day when God might be calling out to us, or are we attempting to use each moment with purpose and gratitude? Each day we have an opportunity to consciously choose to set aside the pursuit of busyness and welcome the gift of time.

Questions

1. Do you identify more with Mary or Martha in this passage?

2. How are you pursuing Jesus amid your busyness?

3. Do you pursue busyness? Are you looking for ways to fill your time?

4. What are some things you do simply to stay busy? How does being busy make you feel?

5. What are some ways you can see time as a gift today?

Jesus Is Rest

"Come to me, all you who are weary and are carrying heavy burdens,
and I will give you rest. Take my yoke upon you, and learn from me,
for I am gentle and humble in heart, and you will find rest for your souls.
For my yoke is easy, and my burden is light."

—MATTHEW 11:28–30

o you ever feel like you can't rest? That you can't afford to escape the work, even for a day? For some it's
hard to stop working. We have a goal for ourselves
or we may feel that achievements define who we are. Maybe we have
something to prove to ourselves or to those around us. There is an
internal race or scoreboard in our minds, and if we take a break, we
may not be able to catch up. We simply can't afford to rest.

From the beginning, the Holy Trinity has been present to remind
us to rest. In the Old Testament, God sets the Sabbath before us as
a reminder to put down our burdens, our work, and our worries.
The seventh day is for rest. In the New Testament, Jesus comes to tell
us we can rest in him. Whether this applies to our personal or our
professional lives, in Matthew 11 Jesus is calling us to rest. He knows
our fear. What if we rest and fall behind? What if we rest and lose
control? What if we rest and don't ever want to get started again?

Jesus doesn't just tell us to rest in Matthew 11. There is a second
part to his statement: *Take on my yoke*. He is not telling us to rest from
all of life's distractions and obligations and then return to the same
commitments of our time once we are refreshed. He's telling us to
permanently rest in him. Jesus isn't just a resting place one day of the

week or twenty minutes a day. Jesus is our resting place all the time. It's hard to imagine resting in Jesus continuously. How do we gain true rest in him?

I think in this case our resting is not just physical but spiritual. Before Jesus arrived on the scene, God's people were bogged down by the law. There was a lot to keep track of, and it seemed like people were having a hard time not only maintaining the law but also agreeing on what the law meant and how it should be carried out. God saw how people were tightly holding on to that law and felt as if they couldn't let go. They couldn't find true rest. They were always worried about doing everything *right*.

Jesus restores rest to us. Sure, we have to work. We have jobs, families, and responsibilities. But we don't have to let those commitments take over. We don't have to allow our work to become our idol. What we do matters, but it doesn't need to be the ultimate, all-consuming, be-all and end-all of our lives. When we truly embrace Jesus' invitation in this passage, when we take on Jesus' yoke, when we rest in him, our accomplishments and failures lose their grip on our identity. If you are truly resting in Jesus, no matter how high or low you may feel, you are the same child of God, called to rest in his yoke.

Questions

1. What is your relationship with work today? Has it always been this way?

2. Do you rest in Jesus? How does this look in your life?

3. How does a good day at your job affect you?

4. How does a bad day at your job affect you?

5. What are ways you can keep perspective on the value of work in relationship to the truth of what Jesus offers?

How We Use Our Time

Treasured Time

"For where your treasure is, there your heart will be also."

—*Luke 12:34*

When we think about treasure, it's common to think about money or possessions. After all, most treasures have some sort of monetary value. It's easy to think that if we aren't overvaluing our retirement and savings accounts or finding security in the things we own, then we aren't treasuring anything more than our relationship with God. But there are plenty of other "treasures" that steal our hearts. And how we spend our time is a significant indication of what those treasures could be. Have you ever taken a personal "time inventory" to reveal where you spend most of your time, to expose what you value most?

In Luke 12, Jesus warns us that the things we treasure are the things that hold our hearts captive. When it comes to our time, this is also true. I know that when I really want something to happen, I take the time to research, plan, schedule, and, essentially, make it happen. I put in the time, focus, and energy because my heart really wants that desire to come about. There are some things within our day that we don't have much control over, but often we can determine what gets a majority of our attention. There's still a lot of time each day or week that is up to our discretion. If we each made a list of the things we do throughout our week and the amount of time we spend on every activity, what conclusion could be drawn about our priorities? Would a stranger reviewing our lists know we were Christians?

I remember several years ago a pastor shared that there were many mornings he found it easier to wake up early and go to the gym rather than getting up early to read his Bible. He reflected on the idea that perhaps this meant he believed the gym offered him more improvement and benefits than God's Word. I found myself convicted by his words. I'm definitely guilty of putting more value on other priorities when it comes to spending quiet time in God's presence. While I would never consciously agree that something can transform me more than the power of God, there are ways I fix my eyes on things throughout my week and treasure more than God simply because I can see or touch these other things. What about you? Are there ways you have created treasures in your schedule that are a higher priority than the Lord? Don't be discouraged! Pray and ask him to reveal these idols. Turn to God and ask him for your heart to be transformed as you plan out your days and weeks ahead.

Questions

1. Take a personal inventory on how you spend your time. What does this reveal to you about your priorities?

2. How could you adjust the ways you prioritize your time in order to put God first?

3. During what season in your life did you wholeheartedly treasure God the most? What habits or routines helped you at that time?

4. What material things or scheduled events do you feel called to release? How do you think it would feel to let go of them?

5. Is there something God is calling you to do in order to draw closer to him?

The Gift of Time

Whatever task you must do, work as if your soul depends on it,

as for the Lord and not for humans.

—COLOSSIANS 3:23

s an introvert, I guard my time. I mentally map out my days and weeks, with the most prevalent concern being, "How much time will I have for myself?" You may be just the opposite and map out how much time you'll have with friends, co-workers, or anyone who is up for being together. I'm not the person who eagerly says yes when someone requests my time. In many ways, tracking how much time I have for myself versus what I offer those around me has made me a time scorekeeper.

There are lots of demands for our time—work, family, friends, exercise, interests, you name it. As my husband and I have become savvier over the years, he and I have started to gift each other time. By sitting down together and looking at the schedule, we try to find pockets of time each of us can use as we please—dinner with a friend, playing sports, or simply being alone in God's presence without distraction. When we look at ways to gift another person time to themselves, it allows us to turn the focus of our personal time toward a more generous spirit of seeing the value of time for those around us.

I have learned that in order to be more generous with my time, I must release the feeling of time entitlement. I need to reorient my view of time, to see it as a gift from God, and this then opens up a creative spark in me that loves gift-giving. While some of us need time to ourselves, I also know it is healthy and freeing to be generous with my time. For those who may be extroverted, the gift of time by yourself and slowing down to hear God's voice may be just the thing your heart truly seeks.

In Colossians 3, the key takeaway is to live and work to honor God, not anyone else. This becomes a clear indicator of how we should be spending our time. When we're not checking in with God, it's easy to say yes or no to different demands on our time based on how we feel. Does it fit into my schedule? Do I want to do it?

When we start seeing our actions as a call to serve God, we ask different questions: Lord, how would you like me to spend my time today? Will this serve those who need to see a glimpse of Jesus? Will this further the kingdom?

Being selfish with our time and "keeping score" might actually prevent God from using us to serve him and others. When we are aware of time as a gift and answer God's call, we are telling him that our time is his to use. A great first step in releasing our grasp on time is to carve out time at the start of each day, asking God what he desires for us. When we set our intention toward him, it allows us to open our plans to him and embrace how he would have us use our time. Ask and listen. Watch and see how God works in mighty ways.

Questions

1. Are you selfish with your time? Why do you tend to guard your calendar?

2. Are you guilty of being a time scorekeeper? When did this begin in your life?

3. Do you spend your time based on what you want or what God wants?

4. How might you change the way you start each day, week, or month?

5. Can you name a time when you did something you didn't want to do but felt it was what God wanted?

Wise with Time

Be careful, then, how you live, not as unwise people but as wise,

making the most of the time, because the days are evil. So do not be foolish,

but understand what the will of the Lord is.

—EPHESIANS 5:15–17

I often equate productivity and efficiency with wisdom. The more efficient I am with my time, the more wisely I'm utilizing my time. The more productive I am in a day, the better I feel in how I spend my hours. That's how my brain operates. Most of us go through our days attempting to get as much done as possible. At the end of the day, we tend to look back with approval for all the things we accomplished, or we look back with disappointment at the lack of productivity in the hours that flew by. While I firmly believe in efficiency, being efficient and being wise are not synonymous. Time can be like an addictive drug if we feel like we never have enough of it. We can get hooked on the adrenaline rush, racing to be as efficient or productive as possible.

But what are we racing toward? When it comes to how we use our time, it's important to resist constantly moving past moments, avoid taking shortcuts at the expense of the experience. When we equate being wise with our time to being efficient or productive, we lose the opportunity to understand the will of the Lord. We suddenly become the center of this universe we've created and we might teeter toward self-centered decisions.

Unfortunately, slowing down and "dethroning" efficiency or productivity is not the answer, either. In doing this we still end up missing the warning found in Ephesians. Instead, God's desire is for his children to slow down but continue to move. We look carefully at our days; we do our best not to rush. We attempt to savor the current hour while also creating a God-inspired future.

The true relationship between wisdom and time is discerning "the will of the Lord." There is a lot to get done each day. What if we made it our daily task to seek wisdom? We may need to accept slowing down; other times it may mean speeding up. When we place God at the center of each day, it may be easier to view time as a gift to be spent wisely.

Questions

1. Do you tend to procrastinate or seek efficiency? What joy do you get from either of these approaches to life?

2. What does being wise with your time mean to you?

3. Are you wise with your time?

4. What things cause you to misuse your time?

5. Do you admire someone who is wise with their time? How do they remain disciplined and consistent with their choices in relation to time? How can you start to incorporate their example into your own relationship with time?

Your Relationship with Time

Not that I am referring to being in need, for I have learned to be

content with whatever I have.

—PHILIPPIANS 4:11

When I speak to groups about God's gift of time, I like to do an interactive exercise with the audience to help participants discover more about their own relationship with time. I ask each person to start by thinking of their relationship with time when they were a young child.

Were you aware of time as a child? Did you have feelings about how you spent your time alone or as a family unit? Were you in control of your time or was someone else organizing how you spent your time?

Then we move on to the teenage years, then early twenties, and finally today's relationship with time. I love this exercise because it allows the participant to recognize their own relationship with time. Many people have not thought about their personal history or associations with time, schedules, and lifelong expectations. Each of our relationships are different, and our stories are unique. I learn a lot about people when we talk about this topic.

When I first started doing this activity with groups, I thought I knew what people would say. I expected everyone to answer like me. But it quickly became apparent that while some did share my experience, others were starkly opposite of my narrative. Asking these questions proved to touch a nerve, and many have been eager to share their perspectives, wrestle with their histories, and make a few changes going forward. Just as our friendships and familial dynamics are individually custom, so is our relationship with time.

The other piece I love about this exercise is that it clearly illuminates the fact that our relationship with time changes as we grow. What we felt as a child is not always what we feel as an adult, and yet this past relationship with time impacts today's decisions.

Philippians 4:11 speaks to contentment in all circumstances. What a lovely goal for each of us. But the key word in this passage is *learned*. Paul states he has learned to be content in all situations. The use of the word "learn" indicates there has been attention, work, and discipline he has directed toward adopting contentment. When we look toward gaining contentment with the time God has gifted us, we must first become aware of how we view and interact with time. Once we do that, then we are able to interact and trust God within our thought process surrounding time. We can invite him into our daily interactions with time. We can pray that even when we feel at odds with time and its constraints, he will reveal his perfect will for each of our days and he will direct us toward contentment with the time we are given.

Questions

1. When you were a child, what was your relationship with time?

2. When you were a teenager, what was your relationship with time?

3. When you were in your twenties, what was your relationship with time?

4. What is your current relationship with time? Think through how it has changed over the years.

5. What are practical ways you can find contentment in your current relationship with time?

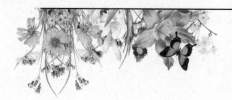

Time Spent Comparing

Do not be conformed to this age, but be transformed by the renewing of
the mind, so that you may discern what is the will of God—what is good
and acceptable and perfect.

—ROMANS 12:2

A s someone who didn't have a lot of friends in the younger years of my life, I had to learn how to entertain myself. While I still maintain a healthy dose of independence, with the over-saturation of social media I've become more aware of what those around me are doing. With technology we are constantly flooded with information: the perfect birthday party someone else is hosting for a 3-year-old, the most amazing educational craft for toddlers, the fantastic vacation someone is enjoying. My friends who are single watch other people's exciting dating life or the party they opted out of, or worse, weren't invited to. There seems to always be something we are missing out on, and it's hard to avoid feeling let down. Fear of missing out (FOMO) is real. Despite the fact that a picture on social media is displaying a few seconds of someone's life, we often let the image of what they're doing infiltrate our expectations of what our lives should look like.

In Romans 12, Paul is telling us not to let comparison or the expectations around us change our purpose or our actions. We must know our needs. Your needs won't be the same as mine, and that's okay. Resist the pressure of comparison from determining your actions. Your abilities, time, and talents are specific to you. When you spend time focusing on the lives of others and how your life may not add up, this can become a serious distraction from what God is calling you to do with your own gifts and talents.

God desires our full attention because he has plans specific for each of us. As a fully loved child of the Almighty, you are the delight of his attention. As God spoke to Jeremiah, "Before I formed you in the womb, I knew you." These words couldn't be more true. Your time is now, and the purpose you were created for is only fulfilled with living in alignment with your heavenly Father today.

It's easy to allow comparison to steal our joy or even persuade us to use our time differently from what God might be asking us to do. When we allow the perceived activities and happiness of others to drive our personal agendas, we are inattentive to God's will for our time and our talents. The next time you find yourself tempted to compare how you are spending your time compared to what your neighbor does, be present and be grateful. Ask God what he desires for you and occupy yourself with his assignment.

Questions

1. In what ways do you compare your life to the lives of those around you?

2. How do you allow the expectations of others to drive your daily decisions?

3. What are some ways you can stop allowing comparison to steal your joy?

4. How do you discern the will of God in your life?

5. In what ways can you quiet unrealistic expectations you have for yourself?

Purpose in Preparation

Prepare your work outside; get everything ready for you in the field;
and after that build your house.

—PROVERBS 24:27

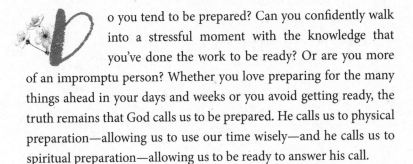

o you tend to be prepared? Can you confidently walk into a stressful moment with the knowledge that you've done the work to be ready? Or are you more of an impromptu person? Whether you love preparing for the many things ahead in your days and weeks or you avoid getting ready, the truth remains that God calls us to be prepared. He calls us to physical preparation—allowing us to use our time wisely—and he calls us to spiritual preparation—allowing us to be ready to answer his call.

When we prepare well, we are able to anticipate the beauty of what is to come. In Proverbs 24, we are told to prepare and then build. That seems like a no-brainer, but then why do we avoid preparation sometimes? Why does God need to remind us of this seemingly obvious truth? Maybe it's because we are selfish with our time. Sometimes preparation, especially spiritual preparation, seems to take us away from things we'd rather be doing. Many times, preparation feels boring. Sometimes when we need to prepare we can feel unseen or even unappreciated by those around us.

Whenever I'm bogged down by the mundane actions of preparation, I try to pray. If the action I am doing is for someone else in my life, I pray for them. The simple task of giving the preparation a purpose beyond the immediate lifts my eyes up and away from myself. Preparation leaves more room for a Spirit-driven encounter.

God calls us to prepare. Our life is arguably one big preparation for eternity. When we treat the smaller moments of our days as opportunities to develop a discipline of preparation, we show respect to the time we have. Some ways God might be calling you to spiritually prepare are through spending time in Scripture and turning to worship music. When we arm ourselves with God's encouragement, it prepares us to follow his lead. When we spiritually equip ourselves, we are more prepared to face our day with grace and truth, even in the face of pain or suffering. When we prepare our hearts to answer God's call there is no limit to how he can use us. How might God be asking you to prepare today?

Questions

1. How do you interact with preparation? Do you tend to prepare for things ahead of time or do you like to wing it? Why do you think that is?

2. Where is one place in your life you could be more prepared? What is one way you could try to be more prepared in this area?

3. How can you find beauty in your moments spent in preparation?

4. How do you think being prepared can assist you in seeing time as God's gift to you?

The Importance of Rest

It is in vain that you rise up early

and go late to rest,

eating the bread of anxious toil,

for he gives sleep to his beloved.

—PSALM 127:2

*H*ave you ever gone on a vacation and felt the relief of stepping away from everything you have to do? Sometimes it takes stepping away from the routine, habits, and "mandatory" schedules of life to see things clearly. Often when we return from a break in routine or vacation, nothing has changed in the demands for our time, but we feel refreshed. We have a new outlook. We are reminded of the blessings around us, even amid full schedules. There is power in stepping away from the daily demands to recover and find balance.

So often we hear the message that we must work harder, be more dedicated, take shorter breaks. Success comes from hard work. I remember watching a successful woman on Instagram talking about how she would wake up at 3 a.m. to start her day and fit it all in as if this was a habit others should take up to be more successful. The message she proclaimed was clear: you have to run yourself ragged if you want to get ahead. But this doesn't align with the message God gives us. Hard work is important, and it does yield results. Yet, hard work without rest often leads to burnout and loss of perspective.

The challenge we face today is to live with margin for the Holy Spirit to work. Many of us need to consciously fight against the pressure to "do more, rest less" that overwhelms our culture. Every body needs rest. And so does every spirit. The challenge becomes not only to create time to rest from physical activity, but also to rest our minds. It's a battle for us to give ourselves permission to *not* get it all done. To not feel guilty for creating physical and mental space absent of productivity that can be measured. But the gift of rest is fortification when we return to the demands in our lives.

Psalm 127 warns us of the danger when we place productivity and success over God's command for us to rest. Nothing we can do on earth can matter more than following God's will for our lives. When we neglect rest, we move in vain. The pressures of this world will never leave us, whether it be parenting, clocking in at the office, or taking care of aging parents. The perspective we gain when we rest restores in us the ability to return to the task stronger than before. And the obedience to God's command to rest restores our understanding of purpose and importance in relation to his almighty glory.

Questions

1. Do you feel the pressure to work harder? Why is that?

2 What is the thing in your life that is hard to break away from in order to find rest?

3. How can you resist the pressure to be more productive at the expense of rest?

4. What happens after you have had time to rest?

5. Have you ever experienced a time when you rested and subsequently felt stronger?

Can We Do It All?

For everything there is a season, and a time for every matter under

heaven: a time to be born, and a time to die; a time to plant, and a time to

pluck up what is planted; a time to kill, and a time to heal; a time to break

down, and a time to build up; a time to weep, and a time to laugh;

a time to mourn, and a time to dance.

—*ECCLESIASTES 3:1–4*

I t's our human condition to want it all. Not only to want it all but to be able to do it all, with little to no help. We are prideful creatures who, if we aren't mindful, can find ourselves trying to do more than we were created to accomplish within the parameters of time.

We can't do it all. Humans weren't built that way. Something always falls through the cracks. It's not because we're not enough. It's not because we aren't trying hard enough. Ecclesiastes 3 states there is a time for every purpose, but it doesn't say that everything should happen at the same time. There is a time for others and a time for yourself. There is a time for cleaning and a time for the mess. There is a time for work and a time for play. When we neglect the holy placement of time in our lives, we forget that all of time has a purpose.

If I were able to do it all, I would miss the importance of time. God didn't create time to remind us of our shortcomings. He gave us time so that we could celebrate, mourn, seek, love, keep, and throw away. There is freedom in our inability to do it all. When we accept that we can't get all of it done, we are able to stay in the moment a bit longer, lingering in contentment. This in turn releases us from the pressure of doing it all and allows us to accept the here and now. But most importantly, our inability to do everything without the constraints of time creates a sacred dependence on the Creator of time. God can do everything beyond the parameters of time. If we were able to do that as well, there would be no need for God. Perhaps, this truth about our own limitations within time is a gift within itself, a gift that takes our inability to get it all done at the same time into a desire toward our heavenly Father—the one who is perfectly able. Through our weakness we are more able to see the perfect beauty of his strength.

Questions

1. Do you feel pressure to do it all? How is that working for you?

2. How do your limitations in what you can do make you feel?

3. What if you only had time for five things today? What would they be? What if you only had time for one thing today? What would that be?

4. Think about a time when your weakness drew you closer to God.

5. How can you release yourself from the pressure to do it all?

6. What encouragement do you find in Ecclesiastes 3?

Time and Technology

So, whether you eat or drink or whatever you do,

do everything for the glory of God.

—1 CORINTHIANS 10:31

As we move forward in time, technology becomes more and more advanced. Technically speaking, technology can refer to any man-made object that helps progress the state of humanity. But most of us think of smartphones, computers, the internet, televisions, and social media when we think about technology in the present age. Every generation has some memory of their own childhood and how today's youth have it easier, or at best different, than a prior generation. The concern of many parents today is that technology is everywhere. Children as young as five are faced with cyber bullying. Screens are distracting our kids from getting outside and playing with friends. But it's not just the youth who are affected by the current advancements in technology.

While there are many great advancements with the digital technology that surrounds us, it takes a toll on each of us. Technology has fostered a society that expects the fastest results we've ever had. We have grown impatient with waiting, thinking everything should be as quick as a click of a button. In some ways, we have lost the art of anticipation. And this type of expectation tends to affect our relationship with God. We don't want to wait. We're programmed to get the next dopamine hit quickly from the pings and dings of computers and phones. And when we send our prayer requests up to Jesus, we tend to expect him to text us back quickly with an answer.

Digital technology often steals our attention and focus away from the things God cares about. While technology in and of itself is not easy to categorize as good or bad, how we use technology can have a dramatic impact on our faith walk. Simply stated, the time we spend interacting with technology can be time away from God's higher purpose for our lives.

First Corinthians 10 reminds us that no matter what we do, we should do it for God's glory. We should take inventory of the time we are investing in social media, streaming movies, playing games, and posting the "perfect" photo. Have you miscalculated your ability to manage your attention span? Have the scales tipped from moderate to unhealthy? Are you consumed with alerts and likes to the point of wasting time?

It's time to simplify. Do everything for the glory of God.

Questions

1. If you were to take an inventory of how much time you spend with digital technology, how much time would it be? Do you think this number is appropriate? Why or why not?

2. In what ways has technology brought you closer to God?

3. In what ways has technology created distance between you and God?

4. Have you seen ways that digital technology and its instant results has made you impatient? Explain.

The Repetition of Time

Again he went away for the second time and prayed, "My Father, if this cannot pass unless I drink it, your will be done." Again he came and found them sleeping, for their eyes were heavy. So leaving them again, he went away and prayed for the third time, saying the same words.

—MATTHEW 26:42–44

Whenever I start hearing the same concept or phrase being repeated in my life, I take notice. Oftentimes there is a lesson or change coming my way, and I begin contemplating how to prepare for what God might have in store for me. God speaks to me in repetition, not only in his Word but through others.

In the Matthew 26, Jesus is in a repetitious cycle with those closest to him. He is instructing the disciples to stay alert with him in these last few hours of the night. The Son goes to his Father, pleading for a pardon. Each time Jesus comes back from prayer, he finds the same thing: sleeping friends. And to make things worse, God doesn't seem to be changing his mind about a really difficult plan that's about to go down.

Repetition might come in the form of running into the same person several days in a row or having different people bring up the same subject matter without knowing it. Sometimes, when I see these repeated themes, I get excited for what's ahead. I love sensing God's interaction in my life. I take comfort in knowing that it's not just me going from choice to choice, but God is in the details. And if something is God-ordained, it's got to feel good, right? Well, no. Not all the time.

There are many repeated signs in our lives that are disappointing or even heartbreaking. Like dating someone who repeatedly shows us he's not capable of commitment. Or sometimes the repetition in life is mundane and just plain disappointing. Dishes needing to be washed. Children asking the same question ten times a day. Laundry on constant repeat. Clocking in at an uninspiring job. Filling the gas tank. Making dinner.

So, what do we take away from Matthew 26? What do we take away from the repetition in life? God never tires of the repeats. He is long-suffering. It's okay to repeatedly approach God when we feel stuck. Even Jesus in his full humanity and deity knows without a doubt that he is going to do what he wishes God would take away. The crucifixion is happening. Just as God resting on the seventh day is for our benefit, Jesus praying three times is done to give us permission to do the same. To encourage us not to give up on crying out, even if it's the tenth or hundredth time doing so.

Whether God is speaking to you through repetition, preparing you for a change ahead, or listening to you cry out about the same thing as last year, don't miss what is waiting ahead by avoiding repetition in your life. Pay attention to what others are saying to you or to the people in your life. Being aware of the repeated concepts allows you to prepare for God's action in real time.

Questions

1. What is God repeatedly telling you?

2. What are you repeatedly telling God?

3. Are you drawn toward or away from repetition? Why do you think you feel this way?

4. What are some ways to see the mundane repetition of our lives as somehow sacred, a calling from God?

5. How do you take comfort from Jesus repeatedly turning to God in Matthew 26?

The Power of Time

Jesus' Time

And Jesus said to her, "Woman, what concern is that to me and to you?

My hour has not yet come." His mother said to the servants,

"Do whatever he tells you."

—JOHN 2:4–5

*H*ave you ever wondered why Jesus arrived at that particular moment in history? If this was God's plan for salvation, why did he wait so long? Why not have Jesus arrive sooner to save the people of the Old Testament? Why let them live under the old covenantal law for as long as they did? And conversely, it's easy to wonder why not have Jesus arrive now? Surely, God can see that social media makes the world a much smaller place. Nothing could more effectively go viral than the Son of God coming to Earth, performing signs and wonders in order to offer himself up as a living sacrifice for humanity.

In John 2 we see one of Jesus' miracles performed, the changing of water into wine. This miracle truly amazed those at the wedding. They didn't understand how the best wine had been left for last. But some weren't amazed because they knew a miracle had been performed. Jesus kept the act of turning water into wine quiet. Jesus was doing the opposite of trying to go viral. He was trying to fly under the radar, avoiding any revelation of his true identity and power. To understand this, we can look to what Jesus said prior to this miracle, "My hour has not yet come." It's likely that what he meant was his time to offer his body as a sacrifice had not yet come.

God knew the exact right time for Jesus to walk this earth and the exact right time to offer salvation through his Son. If Jesus had been born sooner, the people might not have seen a need for him. Everyone could have remained stubborn, thinking, *We can work our way to salvation.* The entire Old Testament is a reminder of who we were before Jesus appeared to fulfill Scripture. There is power in allowing God to offer his perfect way in his perfect time.

What about today? What if Jesus arrived in the present day to show us his radiant glory as the Son of God? Maybe Jesus would go viral with his many signs and wonders . . . or maybe not. In today's society we've become a bit jaded. Technology has allowed for things that would have been considered miracles in the past to be considered normal in today's world. With the advancement of medicine, we might always wonder if it was Jesus who cured the sick or if it was the last dose of chemo. With photo altering, Artificial Intelligence (AI), and special effects, many would think videos featuring Jesus walking on water were simply a new filter on a social media platform. There's so much noise in today's society, would we notice Jesus for who he is? Or would we allow him to blend in with the crowd?

Jesus came at the perfect time. God's knowledge of what should be and what humanity needs transcends time. He is not stuck in any linear pattern. And as a result, God's perfect timing is deliberately chosen with his beloved children in mind.

Questions

1. Jesus tells Mary it is not yet his time when she comes to him for help. Why do you think he decides to perform the miracle of changing water into wine, despite what he says?

2. How does it encourage you to know God brought Jesus to earth at the exact right time in history?

3. Do you see other ways God's timing is perfect in your life? Give examples.

4. What "big questions" cause you to struggle to see God's perfect timing?

5. What do you think would happen if Jesus came to earth today for the first time? Do you think you would recognize him for who he is?

6. How would your faith be affected if Jesus had come earlier in time and the entire Old Testament was not part of Christian history?

Suffering Turned to Hope

And not only that, but we also boast in our afflictions, knowing that

affliction produces endurance. . . . For while we were still weak, at the

right time Christ died for the ungodly. Indeed, rarely will anyone die for

a righteous person—though perhaps for a good person someone might

actually dare to die. But God proves his love for us in that while we still

were sinners Christ died for us.

—Romans 5:3, 6–8

It's tricky to talk about suffering. Suffering is personal.

Often when talking to someone about a hard season they are going through, people will eventually attempt to diminish their suffering by acknowledging that someone out there has it worse than they do. I tend to feel the need to qualify my suffering. Suffering becomes something I have to earn the right to talk about. While it's good to have awareness of other people's circumstances, there is a missed opportunity in sweeping our own suffering under the rug.

God allows us to suffer as a way of purifying our hearts. We can say this because suffering is not the end of the story. We see God's redemption through suffering most clearly on the cross—the cross where Jesus suffered and died for sins not his own. But that isn't the end—he was raised again. His suffering produces hope for all humanity, hope displayed through his resurrection and ascension. But that's God, right? Of course, his suffering produces hope. How can our suffering do the same?

We have a choice every time we encounter any level of suffering in our lives. A choice to become *bitter* or *better*. In today's world it's easy to simplify our daily encounters into the category of purely good or the category of purely bad. Got the job I want—good. Boyfriend broke up with me—bad. But what if that's not how God sees it? What if what we consider "bad" is the good stuff? What if every struggle in life is an opportunity to build character? When we suffer, we have the choice to turn toward something for comfort—food, alcohol, money, television, sex . . . the list goes on. Turning to something other than God in the midst of our suffering will likely produce hopelessness, as these comforts can only ever offer temporary relief. But when we turn toward God and his higher purpose, we can acknowledge that suffering may not be a bad thing in his eyes. Angst and difficulty may be opportunities to deepen our closeness with God and develop complete reliance on him. And if we truly believe in eternal life, in heaven, with our Creator, then we can undoubtedly accept that suffering is not the end of the story.

How do we embrace Romans 5, turning our suffering into hope? We cling to the assurance of who God has been to us in the past. The hope we gain from the cross shows us that God will not leave us in our pain. When suffering is part of our journey, it's an opportunity to be refined and ultimately a gift from God. We all suffer in life. We all have grievances we carry with us. What we do with that suffering highlights our ability and capacity to develop character. If we can remove ourselves from oversimplifying good versus bad categorizations of life here and view suffering as an opportunity to grow, one day Christ will see his clear reflection in us. Cling to hope, even in times of refinement.

Questions

1. How have you experienced suffering in your life? How has your suffering changed you?

2. Where do you find hope in the midst of your suffering?

3. How can you find strength in the power of the cross next time you are experiencing pain in your life?

4. How can you support someone you know who is currently suffering?

3 Days to Rise

For I handed on to you as of first importance what I in turn had received:

that Christ died for our sins in accordance with the scriptures

and that he was buried and that he was raised on the third day

in accordance with the scriptures.

—1 CORINTHIANS 15:3–4

Within the Bible, several numbers have spiritual significance. The number three is one of them. Many believe that the number three references the Trinity—Father, Son, and Holy Spirit. But not only that—the presence of three is thought to be a form of *completeness* in relation to the Trinity. I'm fascinated with this interwoven detail and connection to God's story.

Let's look at three different places the Bible references not just the number three, but specifically three days—Hosea 6:2, Jonah 1:17, and 1 Corinthians 15:3–4. Hosea 6:2 states that the people of Israel will be raised up from their suffering on the third day in order to live before God. Hosea speaks of the Israelites who have abandoned God's instructions. They will not be raised up from physical death, as Jesus is. Instead, they will be raised up from spiritual death, freed from imprisonment and oppression, and released from some cultural assimilations that they likely had embraced over time. When we look at this passage in relationship to 1 Corinthians 15, we see a foreshadowing of Jesus' resurrection. There are significant differences: it is Israel being lifted up in Hosea and Jesus in 1 Corinthians. But in both cases, we see how being lifted on the third day brings a sense of completion in our standing before God.

In Hosea, having God's people lifted up is arguably an imperfect resolution since it involves sinful people, but in the resurrection of Jesus there is perfection, God's faultless Son! Not only is the Trinity complete, but because of Jesus we are welcomed in and can enjoy a beautiful and right standing with God.

In Matthew 12:40, Jesus compares his future death and resurrection to the story of Jonah. Jonah 1:17 tells us that Jonah is in the fish's belly for three days and three nights. At the end of the three days, Jonah prays, confessing his disobedience to God and repenting. It is then that Johan is released from the fish onto dry land. Jonah immediately zeroes in on God's will rather than his own. So, why would Jesus use this reference to foretell his own resurrection?

Jonah's disobedience to God results in three days of imprisonment within the dark, gross belly of a fish—death presses in on every side of Jonah. Likewise, Jesus is imprisoned in death for three days after suffering on the cross. In this case, he is imprisoned for the disobedience of others, not due to any of his own shortcomings. Jesus pays the price of going to death's darkest pit for us. The complete ransom for sin is paid within the span of three days.

Jesus could have risen from the grave at any time. God, in his exact timing of three days, reminds us of his perfect plan and his complete work done through Jesus. At the other side of three days, we see Jesus complete his sacrificial work to join the Father and the Holy Spirit in wholeness.

Questions

1. Why do you think God allowed three days to pass before raising Jesus from the dead?

2. What do you think those three days of separation from God were like for Jesus?

3. How have you seen God fulfill promises to you? Did each instance happen quickly or take more time than you imagined? How did the timing affect your appreciation for the result?

4. Are there other references to the number three in the Bible that come to mind? What can you learn from these examples and passages?

He Will Make Straight Your Paths

Trust in the LORD with all your heart, and do not rely on your

own insight. In all your ways acknowledge him,

and he will make straight your paths.

—PROVERBS 3:5–6

I have had several women approach me about making big changes in their lives. It's hard to step off the well-worn path they are already on. It seems scary. It seems overwhelming. Sometimes it seems risky. Often when we consider making a big change in our lives, we worry that we're stepping off the expected path, the path people around us think we should take. When we start to make a choice that seems to create a crooked trail in our wake, it can be uncomfortable for us and the people around us. It feels as if we have wasted some of our time when we deviate from the plans of the past. I worry that those around me will think I've used my time unwisely when I change my mind. Or I worry that others think the new path ahead will be a waste of time.

When we are fearful about stepping out in faith to make the next right choice, we can look to Proverbs 3 for guidance and encouragement. Verse 5 states that the best decision is to trust in the Lord. When following God's guidance and placing our trust in him, we are never wasting time. Though we may worry that changing our course means we're veering from what we know, verse 6 clearly states that when we are listening to God and walking with him the path is always straight.

This might mean being okay with other people's discomfort. If we're making the right choice for ourselves that is ordained by God, it's okay when others don't like or understand our decisions. Changing our minds is allowed, even when it might seem we have wandered around too long. This doesn't mean we're abandoning wise counsel. It does mean only God can define what is right for our lives. Only he can do that.

There will be many times in life when the path feels crooked, weaving from one direction to the next. But what feels winding to us will always be straight to God. Changing your mind about the direction you want to head, personally or professionally, doesn't mean the time you've spent is wasted. Acknowledging God and intentionally moving closer to his purpose is exactly the path you're intended to take.

Questions

1. Name an instance when you felt that you wasted time. What did you learn from that time?

2. How has God used "setbacks" for a purpose?

3. What is a change you want to make but haven't yet because you are worried about what others will think? Why are you letting this stop you?

4. How do you turn to God before you make big decisions?

5. When you look back on your life, has your path been straight or crooked? Why do you think this?

6. Are you on God's path right now or on your own? What aspects could be improved?

Where Discipline Leads

Now, discipline always seems painful rather than pleasant at the time,
but later it yields the peaceful fruit of righteousness to those
who have been trained by it.

—HEBREWS 12:11

There have been few times in my life when I've regretted being a disciplined person. In the early stages of creating a new discipline, I struggle to do the thing I should do, but gradually over time it becomes less difficult. Often, I even end up enjoying it. Discipline has helped me learn the difference between what I should do and what I want to do. *Should* has taken me on a journey that has transformed me.

The hard thing about being disciplined is that it often feels like you are sacrificing a present comfort for the promise of a future payoff. In order to remain steadfast in the discipline I have found it helpful to be mindful of the beauty or payoff ahead. Often the desire for comfort weakens my dedication to discipline. In these situations, we must challenge our wants—their motives, their truths, and their lies. Despite what the world tells us, our desires are not always good, and getting to the heart of the matter can reveal our own selfish yearnings. Only God's desires are perfect. Many times my desire for comfort will lead me back toward real-time pleasure, away from the fruit of righteousness.

When we attempt to discern the merit of our wants, we can look to Hebrews 12 and ask ourselves if the desire for comfort is keeping us from being disciplined. Not all wants are bad, but sometimes peeling back the layers of desire can lead us toward the future promises of God. In the face of distracting wants that try to pull us from discipline, we can ask ourselves: what is the future payoff? Right now, we may want comfort, but later will we want the result that only comes from discipline?

Having discipline to regularly attend church, actively build community, daily read God's Word, all of these actions might feel challenging at any given moment but will yield heavenly rewards if we stick with it. The best news is that the more we lean into these practices and away from earthly distractions, the easier these disciplines become. God does not expect us to do this by our own strength. He offers us the help and power of the Holy Spirit! If we can make a habit of proper discernment and discipline, we are more apt to hear his soft, still voice and relish the fruit of righteousness.

Questions

1. When has discipline been painful in your life? Why is this?

2. How have you seen discipline lead you to the fruit of righteousness?

3. What do you do because you should? What do you do because you want to?

4. Are you leaning toward present comfort over future fulfillment? Make a list of questions to guide you in godly discernment.

Following the Leader

But Ruth said, "Do not press me to leave you, to turn back from following

you! Where you go, I will go; where you lodge, I will lodge; your people

shall be my people and your God my God. Where you die, I will die, and

there will I be buried. May the LORD do thus to me, and more as well,

if even death parts me from you!"

—RUTH 1:16–17

nfluences surround us. Friends, family, politics, news programs, social media, celebrities, and loads of advertisements: all of these entities are subtly—or not so subtly—swaying us in different directions. Like the air we breathe, we're constantly taking in opinions and persuasions with all five senses. Mindlessly allowing outside pressures to influence our decisions will lead to a destination we might not desire.

In the book of Ruth, we meet a woman who is an example of allegiance at all costs. Ruth has married into a foreign family. Her mother-in-law, Naomi, has lost her husband and her two sons, one of whom was Ruth's husband. Within the first several verses of Ruth 1, we see severe loss and deep-rooted loyalty. Naomi instructs her two daughters-in-law to return to their families. She has no way to provide for them. But in verses 16 and 17 Ruth compassionately resists. As the book continues, we see the beautiful consequences of Ruth's decision: she is able to help provide for herself and for Naomi. Ruth's choice to remain in allegiance to Naomi clearly informs where Ruth ends up.

I have aligned myself with people who have led me down different paths—some helpful, some harmful. I have also been a leader for other people throughout my life, whether I was aware of it or not. Even now as a mother I see that my children are following me, watching me closely, and learning from my words and actions. Our choices matter—whether they are leading those around us or leading us toward our goals. When we allow ourselves to be more aligned with someone on earth more so than being aligned with God, we are likely to be led away from his will for our lives.

Take inventory of the influences in your life and where they might be leading you. Dedicate yourself to God and be influenced by Ruth's allegiance by praying, "Lord, where you go, I will go; who you love, I will love. May I never be separated from your perfect guidance."

Questions

1. What people or influences are most prominent in your life? How do they lead you toward God?

2. What influences tend to lead you away from God?

3. Whom are you leading? Where are you leading them?

4. Think about a time you were misled by someone. What did you learn from this experience?

5. In the Bible God is referred to as the Good Shepherd; how is God shepherding you?

Is Death the End?

"Where, O death, is your victory? Where, O death, is your sting?"

—1 Corinthians 15:55

The end of a good book. The end of a graduate program. The end of a relationship. There are some endings I have looked forward to. There are other endings I have dreaded—or worse, I didn't even see them coming. The end.

All of us deal with endings in our own way. I like to think that over the years, as I have matured, I have hardened myself toward endings. But even now as I think and write about endings my first instinct is to avoid the topic. For some reason endings are predominately sad and painful.

I'm trying to turn that corner, to look at endings as an opportunity, a chance for another beginning. The end of one thing often makes space for the next. There is hope in the end. But I can't ignore the endings that seem cruel. When I think about unwanted endings, death feels like one of the cruelest. Saying goodbye to a loved one can be the most excruciating life circumstance the heart ever faces. Is there hope even in the deepest sorrow?

First Corinthians 15 is a triumphant declaration for believers that death is not the final ending it sometimes feels to be. Jesus conquered the grave. His death and resurrection conquered earthly death in a final battle. Jesus rose triumphant. He is risen. He is alive. Because of his sacrifice made on the cross, Christians can know that on the other side of sorrow hope is waiting. In the most painful endings we lean on God's promise, a hope we can't see, a heaven we might struggle to imagine. And we quiet ourselves with a raw yearning to believe that death is not the end but another beginning.

Time reminds us that when one thing ends, another begins. God created the changing seasons as one of his natural and consistent reminders. Fall is a time when the earth turns inward. Isn't it strange how hope can be born even as we head into a season of death? The seasons gently continue forward, whispering to us that where there is death, there is also new life. Even if beauty is not evident and endings are inevitable, there is always hope.

Questions

1. When you think of endings, what feelings stir within you?

2. Describe a time when an ending turned out to be a positive experience for you.

3. Describe a time when the ending of something was hard for you to process.

4. How do you gain hope from 1 Corinthians 15:55 that even death is not the end because of Jesus?

Waiting on God

Faith in God's Promises

He went in to Hagar, and she conceived, and when she saw that she had
conceived, she looked with contempt on her mistress. Then Sarai said to
Abram, "May the wrong done to me be on you! I gave my slave to your
embrace, and when she saw that she had conceived, she looked on me with
contempt. May the LORD judge between you and me!"

—GENESIS 16:4–5

od doesn't tell us everything at once. Often, he doesn't give us much information to go on at all. That's why we are called to follow him in faith. In Genesis 15, God told Abram (a.k.a. Abraham) that he would father a nation. What an incredible announcement! A dream come true! Abram was in his 80s, and his wife was not much younger. They couldn't believe their good favor. But years went by and still no children. It seemed a little late to start populating an entire nation. But nonetheless that is what God promised.

In some ways it's a very descriptive promise; in other ways a lot of logistical details are left out. If I had just heard from God about my future that held big plans and I played a leading role, my first thought wouldn't be, *Okay, God's got this.* My first thought would be, *How in the world am I going to make this happen?* I've just left a conversation with God, and immediately I'm focused on *me.*

With this in mind, we can start to imagine how Sarai (a.k.a. Sarah) felt in Genesis 16. As Abram shared the promise God stated to him, Sarai was likely thinking, *Surely that promise can't extend to me after all these years.* She is too old! She can't possibly be part of the plan. And like Sarai, some of us have dealt with infertility or the desire to have children when we may not even have a spouse. We know the loss that can come when our bodies don't do what we hope they will or we aren't given the opportunity to try. We can imagine the pain Sarai felt when Abram came home and told her he was going to father a nation. Maybe she had made peace with her infertility. Perhaps it was something she still didn't understand. Either way, she made her own plan when God's message and timeframe didn't add up.

Like Sarai, we make our own plans time and time again. Some of us are so good at making plans, we can forget to even include God in them, let alone ask if they are in line with his perfect will. It's important to seek God's plan before our own in every moment of every day. It seems silly sometimes to ask God what his plan is for our day when it feels like we're doing mundane or insignificant tasks. Dropping off kids, working out, meeting with friends, going to work—all these activities feel too mundane to bring before God. But when we stop asking God what his plan is, we start thinking it's all up to us. We no longer lean on the grace and power of God. We are doing things our way.

Sarai heard Abram say he would have a baby, and she didn't sit back and say, "Wow, I can't wait to see how that's going to happen." Instead, she grabbed the closest fertile woman and said, "I can make this happen."

How many times have you heard a promise from God and attempted to take control of it? Stop making your own plans and expecting God to join in. Start seeking his plan first and wait. If listening becomes your starting point, when the Almighty speaks of an inconceivable plan for your future, instead of asking, *How will I ever do that?* you will say, *I can't wait to see how God will make this happen.*

Questions

1. In what areas of your life are you tempted to do your own thing instead of waiting on God's plan? Why?

2. When have you received a promise from God and doubted his ability to make it happen?

3. How have you seen God use ordinary moments of your day to deliver joy or bring comfort?

4. What is the biggest obstacle to confidently trusting God's plan for your life at all times?

5. What is something you gave up on but God still made happen?

You Cannot Stop God's Plan

God said, "No, but your wife Sarah shall bear you a son, and you shall name him Isaac, I will establish my covenant with him as an everlasting covenant for his offspring after him. As for Ishmael, I have heard you; I will bless him and make him fruitful and exceedingly numerous; he shall be the father of twelve princes, and I will make him a great nation."

—GENESIS 17:19–20

We make decisions daily. Sometimes we make decisions with God and sometimes we make decisions without God. When we make decisions with God, we are adhering to God's intentions, submitting to his will. When we go our own way, we are sending the message: *I am the master of my time, I decide how and when things get done.* You would think that God would abandon us every time we show our defiance, but praise God, this isn't the case. He sees us as his children even when we get off track or full of ourselves. He continues to work all things for good. We can't get in the way of God's plan.

Abraham and Sarah heard God's promise but took matters into their own hands. Abraham and Sarah deviated from God's plan in a major way. Ishmael was born of Hagar, Sarah's maidservant. Ishmael was born as a result of frustration and impatience. Even in the midst of unfaithfulness, God remained faithful. He didn't forsake Abraham and Sarah because of their choice. In Genesis 17, God revealed his plan of redemption. God didn't say "never mind, this is beyond my help." God came near, interacted, and repeated his intentions; Abraham and Sarah were still his beloved followers. God reiterated his covenant stating he would still use them for his purpose.

Abraham and Sarah aren't the only biblical examples of God's mercy in the face of defiance. Adam and Eve ate the fruit, and though God removed them from the garden, he didn't remove them from his presence or plan. Moses struck the rock to pour out water rather than speaking to it as commanded. While Moses would never enter the Promised Land, God continued to love him and use him to establish the Israelite nation. The Israelites doubted God repeatedly, but they remain his chosen people.

The character arc of every human story is redemption. I take comfort knowing I can't get in the way of God's plan. This doesn't mean I should move blindly and without tact as I make decisions in the world. Instead, it reassures me that I am never beyond redemption. There is no choice I can make in life that will separate me from the love of God. There isn't a moment in time that that is beyond his sovereign hand. Even when we work in direct opposition to God's plan, he is always working to bring us back to him.

Questions

1. Give an example of a time you put your own plan above God's plan. What happened?

2. How have you seen God's redemption in your life?

3. When have you stepped out in faith? How did you see God meet you there?

4. When have you thought you were following God's will but were then redirected by God?

For Such a Time as This

"For if you keep silent at this time, relief and deliverance will rise for the
Jews from another place, but you and your father's family will perish.
Who knows? Perhaps you have come to royal dignity
for just such a time as this."

—ESTHER 4:14

In the history of this world, we are not that important. But we want to be. We want our time to matter. And we can get caught up in our own agendas. There is an undeniable struggle to protect our reputation, our finances, and certainly our precious time on earth. Sometimes we rush from one activity to the next, acting as if the world will crumble if we let the ball drop. It's easy in the commotion of our day to consider anything unexpected as interruptions to how we should be spending our time. We might begin to view disturbances of our agenda as events or people getting in the way of our importance. We want to be viewed as important, as having value. But how often are we rushing through the day, shooing away people and other things we've deemed interruptions?

Many of us are looking for our big moment. We want to stand out "for such a time as this." But not everyone experiences that "big moment." Esther's story is not our story. And having a big breakthrough with public recognition may not be what God is asking us to do. God calls us to the everyday. Each morning he whispers, "For such a time as this." He longs for us to respond to his calling and see each day as a distinct moment that will never occur again. It's easy to miss. For some of us most days feel a bit like a scene from the iconic

– 159 –

film *Groundhog Day*. Wake up, survive, go to bed, then do it all over again the next day.

But each day isn't the same; it's uniquely made by a very creative and imaginative God. Each day is distinct. And our importance is rooted in God's Word, not public recognition. Our challenge is to discover the opportunity in each day. Whether our "for such a time as this" is a big moment or a small occurrence, it's deliberately placed in our path. It's a call from God, asking for a response. It's a divine appointment to make a contribution.

God's great work will happen with or without us. This is made perfectly clear in the first part of Esther 4:14, "For if you keep silent at this time, relief and deliverance will rise for the Jews from another place." God doesn't need us. He doesn't need our interaction to have his will accomplished. But there are things that only you are being asked to act upon—asking the woman at Bible study if she is okay, offering to help a stranger in need, taking a meal to a new mom. Will you answer the call or will God find someone else to ensure things happen, with or without you? We can't stop God's perfect timing. God doesn't need you; he invites you. Your response to his request will be enough. In fact, he takes delight in you.

Questions

1. Do you seek importance in your daily life? What does that look like?

2. What are the small opportunities God is offering to you in making a difference? How can you respond to his calling?

3. When have you refused to do something God called you to do?

4. Did you see his plan happen without you?

5. From whom do you seek recognition for your contributions?

6. How do you define *significance*? Does this align with Scripture?

Waiting for the Right Time

Wait for the LORD; be strong, and let your heart take courage;

wait for the LORD!

—PSALM 27:14

inding the right time usually means waiting. We wait on a lot of things in our lives. It's easy to grow impatient in the waiting. We find ourselves thinking, *I'd be okay with the waiting as long as I knew it was all going to work out.* We want assurance that it's going to be fine. Sometimes we clearly hear him making a promise to us but we aren't sure when or how it will come to pass. Other times we feel stuck, waiting to even hear God's voice.

Though it might feel like waiting is our enemy, waiting allows us to prepare for the unknown. It stirs anticipation and might even create a yearning for what's to come, even if pain and disappointment are in our future. Waiting allows us to turn toward God, developing a trust in him rather than ourselves. In reading through the Bible, I have learned that when I pursue something outside of God's timing, it almost always blows up in my face.

It's not easy to identify God's time, the right time. That's part of the mystery of God and having faith. He purposely doesn't give us the entire, detailed roadmap to life. Can you imagine how less exciting it would be if we knew exactly what would happen? We would miss out on valuable wisdom that comes from the ups and downs of each experience.

Psalm 27 is a clear notice to every believer who wants all the answers up front—wait on the Lord! What's interesting is that in verse 14 the word "courage" is used. Often, we think of waiting as passive, but it doesn't have to be. The use of courage in this verse reminds us that there is action in waiting. We are honing our skills of patience. We are turning our attention toward God by seeking out wise counsel, reading God's Word, and fervently praying.

Just like time, waiting is a gift from our heavenly Father. There is no room for hope if we know everything that is to come. There is no dependence on God if he gives us the answers up front. God yearns for a deep and meaningful relationship with his children. Wait with courage.

Questions

1. How do you feel about waiting?

2. When have you been confident of God's timing in your life? How were you able to discern this?

3. What answers would you like God to give you about your life?

4. Recall a time you when waited well. What happened?

5. Think of a specific Bible story or biblical character you can turn to as an example of waiting on God. Read that story again to refresh your recollection of the details.

40 Years of Wandering

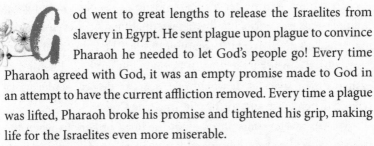

"I am the LORD your God, who brought you out of the land of Egypt,

out of the house of slavery; you shall have no other gods before me.

You shall not make for yourself an idol, whether in the form of anything

that is in heaven above or that is on the earth beneath or that is in

the water under the earth."

—EXODUS 20:2–4

od went to great lengths to release the Israelites from slavery in Egypt. He sent plague upon plague to convince Pharaoh he needed to let God's people go! Every time Pharaoh agreed with God, it was an empty promise made to God in an attempt to have the current affliction removed. Every time a plague was lifted, Pharaoh broke his promise and tightened his grip, making life for the Israelites even more miserable.

It's believed that the Israelites endured Egyptian slavery for at least 350 years. For 350 years, the Israelites lived under the authority of a foreign ruler. For 350 years, the Israelites were living amongst a culture different from their own. There were behaviors and societal norms that the Israelites adopted while in captivity. No matter how faithful they were to God, it's likely that some spiritual and cultural lines were blurred. Just think about how hard it is to live in today's society and remain faithful to God. We feel like we can manage and maintain our faith walk, but honestly, it can be that much easier to assimilate our lifestyle with ungodly patterns. How often do we blend in with non-Christians around us?

When Pharaoh finally released the Israelites from slavery, God led them on an exciting journey toward the Promised Land. But as people do when they move into an unknown situation, the excitement wore off and it quickly became a longer trail than any were expecting. The Israelites wandered the desert for 40 years—that's a long time! Why would God—the God of deliverance—take so long to bring the Israelites to a settled home?

In Exodus 20, God provided the Ten Commandments. His first commandment was to only worship God. This seems simple enough, but the Israelites had been surrounded by pagan worship for generations. Remember the 350 years in Egypt part? Worshiping multiple gods was normal to them; they might not have even realized many had come to accept it as a way of life. The habits and beliefs "normalized" during their time in Egypt could not be left behind as easily as their shackles. It would take years of desert wandering to rebuild dependence and trust in the one true God.

We see several times throughout the book of Exodus when the Israelites beg to go back to slavery! If they had been delivered to their new neighborhood too quickly, they might have set up new homes with old habits. God did not have the Israelites wander for 40 years without a purpose. He wanted time with his people. And he does not let you wander in what feels like the wilderness without a purpose either. God uses time to sanctify us. Consider his perfect timing the next time you feel like you're wandering and wondering.

Questions

1. What habits do you think you have adopted from today's culture that are at odds with your faith? How can you work to release these habits to walk in obedience toward God?

2. If you had been an Israelite wandering in the wilderness, what do you think you would have felt?

3. Has there been a time God has made you wait longer than you wanted for relief? Why do you think he chose this timing?

4. How are you being obedient to the command in Exodus 20:2-4? How are you being disobedient?

The Wrong Time

The LORD is good to those who wait for him, to the soul that seeks him.

It is good that one should wait quietly for the salvation of the LORD.

—LAMENTATIONS 3:25–26

After my second miscarriage, one right after another, I didn't get pregnant again for seven months. I was grieving and struggling with understanding God's timing. I couldn't keep a baby alive, and I couldn't conceive another. Some months were easier than others, but many times I was all too aware of the deficit. I was in a season of waiting that butted up to a season of mourning. It was brutal.

Fertility issues aside, the months of waiting were generally hard months for our family. We were in a state of transition and having trouble working well together. Ben and I couldn't seem to communicate effectively, and this led to arguments and frustrations. It was a very difficult summer. I couldn't clearly see God's plan, but as we worked through some of our challenges (and came out a stronger team), I started to see the beauty in the losses we had suffered.

If I had not lost both pregnancies, I would have been very pregnant in the midst of many other strains we faced, possibly causing toxicity in different ways. If I had gotten pregnant during our strenuous summer, it might have added pressure to other fragile relationships. I can see all this now. I can see God's mercy in what came to pass. I can see the beauty of waiting on God's timing. I can see this on the other side of developing my patience. But sometimes it's just plain hard to see while you're in the thick of things.

What happens when I don't wait well? I take things into my own hands. I make decisions outside of God's life-giving guidance. I make mistakes. Oftentimes I wonder if I'm waiting well or giving up. Thankfully God can use my mistakes and my misgivings; he knows my frailty and is faithful even when I am faithless.

Have you lost track in your waiting? Have you settled for something that is "less than"? It's easy to abandon waiting for a compromise. After all, there is no guarantee you will get what you want in this life. Sometimes there is an end to your waiting. Sometimes there isn't. But God is with you in what might feel like the waiting room. He will guide you toward patient decisions rather than impatient compromises. His salvation endures.

Questions

1. How might you see failures in your life as opportunities to grow?

2. What signs and emotions do you recognize when something is not God's timing?

3. How is waiting an action verb in your life?

4. Name several events in nature that take time to happen (such as flowers blooming).

5. What are you waiting on for God's direction? Write a prayer to ask God for his perfect timing.

That's Not How I Do It!

Then Jesus called his disciples to him and said, "I have compassion for the crowd because they have been with me now for three days and have nothing to eat, and I do not want to send them away hungry, for they might faint on the way." The disciples said to him, "Where are we to get enough bread in the desert to feed so great a crowd?"

—MATTHEW 15:32–33

Thats *not* how I do it!" is a common phrase I find myself repeating over and over again. Sometimes I say it to the people around me but most times I say it to God. Each of us has habits we've developed throughout our days. We have preferences regarding how we like to accomplish tasks, spend our time, and treat others. We have opinions about how things should be done, and, in many ways, this makes sense. But many times our opinions about how things should be done and how much time it should take to do them are more about our desires than about God's desires. I've learned over the years (and continue to learn) that how I do things is as unique as my fingerprints. But just as my routines can be a strength, they can also be a weakness.

When we read the Gospels, we see many signs and wonders performed by Jesus. Matthew 15 is just one example of our Lord's power. And yet, not all believed him to be capable. Jesus' own followers were confused when it came to Jesus wanting to feed a crowd. They found him to be illogical and confounding. Even though the disciples had God's Son standing right in front of them, healing the sick, walking on water, and multiplying food, they still asked him "How?" and "Why?"

Jesus did things the way he knew best. His disciples still questioned and doubted. They forgot the miracles of the past when faced with a problem of the present. Just one chapter earlier in Matthew 14, Jesus multiplies food to feed 5,000, yet when it comes time to do it again, the disciples ask where they will get enough food to feed the crowd. They ask because Jesus does things dramatically differently than they do.

I can't think of a time when I've told God, "That's *not* how I do it!" and had an easy go of it. Can you? God's plan is never substandard to our own plan. Still, we keep finding ourselves telling him how he should work things out—and we assume we're right! The most grace-giving part of this exchange is that even when we try to strong-arm our way forward, God always lovingly leads us back to him.

It feels foolish and shortsighted, maybe even blind to forget all he has done before and not trust him for all that lies ahead. Are we not picking up where the disciples left off? It's tempting to read the Bible and think, *How could Jesus' disciples not see what was right before them?* Funny how that works when you're looking through a lens of completion. We know the whole story. We've seen Christ's actions from birth to ascension and can make sense of his ministry. Maybe it's time for me to stop saying, "That's *not* how I do it!" and proclaim, "Let's see how God's going to do this!"

Questions

1. How are you assuming you know God's plan or telling him what to do?

2. How can you choose to obey rather than attempt to lead?

3. When have you forgotten the promises of God? What helped you remember them?

4. How do you relate to the disciples in Matthew 15?

5. Jesus said, "I have compassion for the crowd," and was moved to help them. How might you lead with compassion more often?

Stop Hiding

"He has told you, O mortal, what is good,

and what does the Lord require of you but to do justice and

to love kindness and to walk humbly with your God?"

—Micah 6:8

There is a difference between waiting and hiding. While we're waiting it's important to discern the right time for action. Sometimes we say we're waiting to make a change, waiting for the right time, waiting for God's guidance, but in fact we aren't really waiting, we're hiding. Maybe we started off with good intentions, but after a while we got comfortable. We stopped perking our ears up for God's call to move and we settled in, probably stagnant and most likely wasting the gift of time.

It can be hard to know when waiting turns into hiding. You may be in a job you've dreamed of leaving for years. Maybe you're in a relationship that doesn't seem to be going anywhere. You want to be healthier and more fit, but you keep sitting on the couch rather than choosing movement and whole foods. I've learned that when my words don't align with my actions this is my first clue that I might be hiding. Hiding is a deterrent to action. In hiding, we might even be comfortable saying, "I'm waiting for God," rather than taking a step forward ourselves. In hiding, we're likely ignoring the loving nudges that he sends our way. In hiding, we neglect using time for God's fullest purpose.

When your waiting becomes passive, perhaps it has stopped being waiting and has turned into hiding. If you find yourself stuck in a pattern of hiding, a great way to combat the inaction is to start saying *yes*. Yes to one or two opportunities that come your way. By saying yes, you'll open your mind and heart to where God might be leading rather than staying stuck in inactivity.

Looking to Scripture for encouragement we see that Micah 6 is filled with action words—do, love, walk. Waiting doesn't equal passivity. In fact, sometimes waiting means putting forth more intentional thought, attention, and conscientious actions on our end. In Micah 6 we are told that God commands us to do justice, love kindness, and walk humbly. When we obey God's loving instruction, we move confidently out of hiding. We understand that even waiting produces fruit. With eyes forward and with hopeful expectation, we trust his will for our time on earth is being completed.

Questions

1. In your own words, what is the difference between waiting on God and hiding from God?

2. What area in your life might be a place of hiding?

3. What area in your life is a place of waiting?

4. What is one thing you've been declining that you might need say yes to?

5. List a few examples of how you are walking with God in your day to day.

Jesus' Return

"But about that day and hour no one knows,

neither the angels of heaven, nor the Son, but only the Father."

—Matthew 24:36

When is Jesus coming back? Just as we might wonder why Jesus was born 2,000 years ago, we likely have questions surrounding his second coming. It seems to be a popular notion in the present day to predict when Jesus will return. It's fascinating to read different predictions that have bubbled up over the centuries. Many people today look at news headlines and alarming weather patterns and claim that surely these events point to Jesus' impending arrival.

The book of Revelation is chock-full of clues as to what it will be like upon Jesus' return. General timelines and indicators are reported by the Apostle John in graphic detail. But even John's vision doesn't tell us the exact date or time. Jesus himself says, "only the Father knows." In Revelation 22:12, Jesus uses the word "soon" when he speaks of his coming. And in fact, many of the disciples went about spreading Jesus' message after his death with a sense of urgency. When we read the New Testament, we see language and even some life instructions that indicate the disciples were expecting Jesus to return within their lifetime.

If a day is like a thousand years and a thousand years are like a day (2 Peter 3:8), do we hold on to the urgency expressed in the New Testament? Do we really hang our hats on the word "soon" when God is above time? I can say with assurance that what is soon to God does not feel soon to me.

Over the years, I've come to believe that God wants us to hold our faith with the same sense of urgency the disciples did. It helps me to compare this scenario with having really amazing friends come to our home. I may be unsure of their exact arrival time, but I'm excited to prepare my home with care and speed, wanting everything to be ready for their arrival. I'm driven by happiness, thinking of the time we'll share in one another's company. I stay alert to the sounds outside, cars passing, doors opening and closing, reflections of light. I peek out the window checking for their arrival. Sometimes I even wait on the front steps, watching the horizon of our little street, or I'll tell people about our plans and how excited I am. It's this same eagerness and energy in our hearts that we can nurture and stoke for Jesus' known arrival.

Many of us would like to know when Jesus will return—at least tell me if it's during my lifetime! But the truth is, we won't know. We can only prepare ourselves, anticipate his return, ruminate on God's instructions, share God's invitation with those we meet, and watch with sheer excitement and expectation.

Questions

1. How would knowing the time of Jesus' second coming change your behavior in the present moment?

2. The disciples expected Jesus to return quickly. How do you think they felt when he did not come back when they thought he would? How would you feel? What do you think helped the disciples keep the faith when God didn't do what they thought he would?

3. Are you eager for Jesus' return? Explain why or why not.

4. In what ways are you preparing your heart for Jesus' arrival?

5. What helps you maintain your faith?

Don't Forget
the Journey

Love the Moment

Let all that you do be done in love.

—1 CORINTHIANS 16:14

I t's easy to stop being present in every moment of your day. While each minute is given to us with intention, sometimes it seems like there is a lot of "down time"—moments that have no significant purpose. If you're like me, you spend time counting down minutes to the next appointment, "waste time" on your phone as you wait for an activity to begin, or get lost in thought while waiting at the grocery checkout. If we aren't careful, we can easily stop being present as we move through our days. We stop seeing beauty (or even other human beings!) when we're doing anything "less than" what we deem important. We check out of the moments we consider ordinary. Every now and then, I'm so focused on getting through the day that when I snap out of it, I realize I missed out on simple things: my child's laugh, blooming flowers, a beautiful sky, or the smell of clean laundry.

Our lives can feel complicated. They are filled with ups and downs, successes and failures. Sometimes these highs and lows feel well balanced, and sometimes they sway in one direction, tipping the scales. If we notice we have stopped being present within our days we can look to 1 Corinthians 16:14, "Let all that you do be done in love." When you read these words it can seem like a simple instruction. But the truth is, there are many things we do that we don't love. There are many things we do because we have to. How do we honor God's words in the dull moments of our day when it feels easier to check out?

We do all things with love. It sounds oversimplified, and the truth is we might not be able to do all things with love, but we can try. After all, God doesn't ask for our perfection, he asks for our hearts to turn toward him and be softened to his ways. He asks us to try to the best of our abilities and with the help of the Holy Spirit. We can seek love in everything we do.

Try this exercise today when you find yourself spending your time in a way that is boring or not what you want to be doing. Repeat a paraphrase of 1 Corinthians 16:14 to yourself: "All that I do today, may it be done in love." If you are in the last hour of work, pray for a co-worker as you finish your tasks for the day. If you are working out at the gym, praise God for the ability to move your body. If you are soothing a child, thank God for the gift of life.

Even in the moments when love isn't evident, we can be looking. If we seek love, we're paying attention. We probably won't notice every detail of every day. But we can start to bring awareness to our surroundings and recognize how we are interacting with the time we are given. You may even notice particulars that might otherwise have gone unnoticed. When we're able to see the beauty in the details of our day, we're present.

Questions

1. In which moments of your day do you struggle to stay present to the gift of time?

2. What are distractions that block you from appreciating the beauty around you?

3. What is one area of your week where you feel called to bring 1 Corinthians 16:14 into your thoughts, to do all things with love?

4. Using all five senses is a great way to signal to our minds that we are present. Try closing your eyes and noticing the sounds around you. What do you hear, smell, feel? When you are struggling to find something to love in your day how can you use your senses to help bring you close to God's delights?

Vanity Steals Time

Do not adorn yourselves outwardly by braiding your hair and

by wearing gold ornaments or fine clothing; rather, let your adornment be

the inner self with the lasting beauty of a gentle and quiet spirit,

which is very precious in God's sight.

—*1 Peter 3:3–4*

 hen I was twenty-eight, I gave up looking in the mirror for Lent. I was single and living alone. Forty days without seeing my reflection. I covered all the mirrors in my home and avoided even seeing my reflection in the toaster. As you can imagine, the first week of this was a steep learning curve. I learned to put my makeup on blindly. I dried my hair without seeing the finished product. And I never knew exactly how my outfits really looked. Pictures were taken of me during that time, and I never saw them. It was strange and wonderful all at the same time. Although I felt disoriented in the beginning of my mirror-fast, by the end I felt freed. Many times, our perception of ourselves comes from a reflection. That minute we spend in front of a mirror can dramatically change our self-confidence.

When Lent was over and my reflection returned, I found I was once again distracted by the person looking back at me. *Do my knees always look that way?* I even went so far as to enlist a few friends in assessing my legs when we were out to dinner one night. More minutes wasted on worrying about my appearance.

First Peter 3:3–4 is a tricky verse to take in. Most of us have braided our hair, and many of us wear jewelry and pay some attention to the clothes we wear. Are we being disobedient to the Scripture? I don't think wearing jewelry or braiding our hair or buying a new pair of jeans is inherently evil. But vanity and pride are. When how we look becomes our idol, it robs us of our peace. It distracts us from the moment, stealing our time and stealing our joy. If we could focus more on how we feel rather than how we look, the moments and memories would be so much sweeter.

We are reminded in verse 4 that the most important adornment we can have is in our spirit. We are to pay the most attention to what lies within each of us—a gentle and quiet spirit. The most valuable time we can spend is adorning our spirit. Kindness, humility, and listening to others are examples of the characteristics that grow when we foster gentle and quiet spirits. Everyone, no matter their exterior, houses a spirit that is waiting to be cared for and drawn closer to its Creator.

Vanity is a thief of our time. It's easy to get wrapped up in the presentation of our lives—our bodies, our image on social media, our homes. Do we know the "right" people at church? Are our kids behaving? How do our arms look? We care about what others think. We have our own expectations for our lives. The best way to stop allowing vanity and pride to steal more of your time is to adorn your soul through time in Scripture, fellowship with God, and serving others. The truth is, God made each of us with intention. We are his beautiful creations, made in his image. When the mirror threatens to distract or beckons us to waste time worrying about our exterior, rest in the truth that our earthly bodies are for a season, but our souls are for eternity—eternally lovely.

Questions

1. In what ways are you distracted by worrying about your appearance?

2. How would a month without mirrors make you feel? What would you appreciate about this experience?

3. How are you nurturing a gentle and quiet spirit?

4. Name a few people from your life's journey who have inner beauty. What qualities of their personality or spirit are attractive to you?

5. In what ways are you focusing on the beauty of your soul?

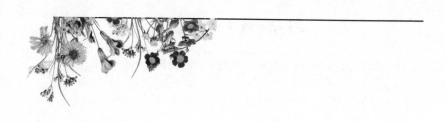

Finish Lines

For I am convinced that neither death, nor life, nor angels, nor rulers,

nor things present, nor things to come, nor powers, nor height, nor depth,

nor anything else in all creation will be able to separate us from

the love of God in Christ Jesus our Lord.

—ROMANS 8:38–39

*T*here are many things that yield happiness throughout our lives. Test scores, college degrees, accolades from work colleagues, friend groups, an ideal physique, clothing, retirement savings, even our children's accomplishments. This seems to be what humans do. We gravitate toward things to "complete" us and bring us joy. This desire to strive and acquire things often causes us to be impatient or rush toward what we imagine will make us whole. And yet these things will never make us permanently happy or satisfied. We're left looking to the next thing once we've reached a particular goal. This is our earthly bent, to try and fill the God-sized hole in our hearts with earthly possessions or accomplishments.

There are many perceived finish lines in our lives, destinations that we are traveling through time to reach with eagerness, hoping they will make us feel complete or satisfied. Too bad they never do. It can be disheartening to recognize this nature within us, this yearning and impatience to reach for satisfaction from things in this world rather than God. Romans 8 offers us hope as we combat racing toward earthly desires: nothing can separate us from the love of God. Just as nothing can fill our hearts like God can, nothing will permanently separate us from his redeeming love either.

With this good news we are able to put any earthly finish lines into perspective. We can understand that no one thing on earth is going to fix everything in our life. No one thing will make us perfectly whole or satisfied. If we are able to take a step back from our goals and desires to see them for what they are, we are able to disarm them. And by disarming them, we are able to remain content, enjoying the time it takes to reach a goal just as much as actually attaining it. Balance and true joy are found in knowing our value and identity are not changed by accomplishments; we have value because we were created by a God with inexpressible worth.

The only true finish line is God. We all have a limited number of days on this planet. We will have good moments and bad. We will achieve and fail. If we can accept that none of our successes or failures will change our finish line—an eternity with God—then we can rejoice and embrace all parts of the process. Rather than rush to the next item on our list and depend on our goals to produce lasting happiness, we can delight in God's never-ending, never-breaking, always-present love.

Questions

1. Is there a goal that makes you think, *Once I have attained that, then I'll be happy?*

2. What are some of life's experiences you are proud of and thankful you've been able to enjoy?

3. If God is our reward and final destination, how does this change your goals and behaviors today?

4. How does the proclamation of Romans 8:38–39 make you feel?

5. Name a failure that ultimately brought you closer to God.

The Language of Time

Let the words of my mouth and the meditation of my heart
be acceptable to you, O LORD, my rock and my redeemer.

—PSALM 19:14

The easiest way to take inventory of our relationship with time is to consciously note the language we use throughout our day. Are we celebrating the time we had each day or are we berating ourselves—maybe even complaining to others—that we didn't have enough time? Psalm 19:14 reminds us that it's not just our actions that matter, it's our words and our inner thoughts and feelings. Are we speaking about the time we are gifted with gratitude or are we constantly grumbling about time? Think about the words you speak in relation to your schedule, meetings, playtime, bedtime, setting an alarm, etc. How do these words shape your thoughts or impact your attitude? What is God hearing you say about time?

When I did this exercise, I realized I spoke negatively about time in front of my children, underscoring the idea that time was the enemy or something we had to beat. I realized my "self talk" about time caused me to constantly feel like I was failing. It's easy to slip into a pattern of language that leads us away from honoring time. With every word we think or speak we have a choice in how we guide our hearts. Words can build or tear down. When we use negative words to express our feelings about the time we are gifted we start to devalue time. We might even label time as an obstacle to our divine calling. When we see time as an obstacle, we get upset when things don't go the way we want them to go. We may see ourselves as victims of time, rather than benefactors of time—as if things are happening to us and we have no power to change the outcome. *Tired, rushed, too busy, ran out of, didn't get enough*—these are just some examples of words we might causally throw around, not realizing they're breaking down our relationship with time. When these words become repeated and well-worn presences in our lexicon it might be time to examine our hearts.

Every minute, we have a choice. We have options regarding our attitude, attention, actions, and words. Though many of us are tempted to feel like victims now and again, the truth is with God, we are never victims. With God we are empowered to live into the purpose he gave each of us. While we might have to participate in demands on our time that we don't always wish to—caring for sick family members, doctor's appointments, overtime at work—we still have options. Walk and speak with confidence as you contemplate your relationship with time. Choose positivity in your thoughts and words. Look for opportunities to use honoring words when it comes to time.

Questions

1. What are the things you view as obstacles in your day? How can you change your thoughts and language around these activities?

2. Take inventory: What are the words of your mouth revealing about your relationship with time? What are your words showing about the meditations of your heart?

3. What areas of your day do you feel you have choices in how you spend your time? What areas of your day do you feel you don't have choices?

4. What words/ideas could you use to replace words/ideas like "busy" or "not enough time"?

Resist Regret

"Is this not the very thing we told you in Egypt, 'Let us alone so that we can serve the Egyptians'? For it would have been better for us to serve the Egyptians than to die in the wilderness."

—EXODUS 14:12

ime is a linear creation. At any given moment, you can only experience one place in time, and from that one place you either look forward to the future or behind you to the past. It's also true that we are never fixed in one place within the element of time. We are constantly moving forward to the next moment with every tick of the clock. Time is unyielding in its nature. This continuous motion—being propelled into the next moment— can sometimes have the strange effect of causing us to look backward far too long. If we remain backward focused, the feeling of regret settles in.

When we are stuck feeling regret, doubt becomes its companion. Regret clouds our ability to see God's perfect plan. Regret can make us doubt God's guidance and his intentionality. Satan loves this. He wants us to be so caught up in the past that we stop being attentive to God's call in the present, and this doubt even dims the prospects of the future.

Exodus 14 warns against looking back with regret. For context, the Israelites have just escaped slavery in Egypt. God performed many miraculous works to free the Israelites from Pharaoh's grip. And yet, while Pharaoh pursues the Israelites, wanting them to come back, God's people reveal their hearts are fearful and stuck in looking back at what they had before the exodus. Their regret in following Moses reveals their distrust in what God has promised and is leading them toward.

Regret steals your attention from the present. Regret wastes time. When we are focused more on past decisions or dreaming up an alternate outcome, we miss the joy waiting for us in the current moment. Sometimes we miss the joy of weeks or months! Exodus 14 isn't the only record of the Israelites looking back in regret. There are many times during their trek in the wilderness that God's chosen people claim they'd prefer to return to Egypt and a life of slavery rather than trust God in the present. Isn't that what regret is at its most basic level: telling God we don't trust him? And he isn't capable of redeeming past choices we've made?

God is our redeemer—past, present, and future. He allows us to be made new through the grace of his Son. As we live in the truth of our Christian faith—that nothing is beyond God's perfect provision—we must release the temptation to look back and feel regret. God calls us to a higher place, looking forward with hope and confidence, living every moment filled with trust and joy that only he can he offer.

Questions

1. How has regret robbed you of a present joy?

2. What do you learn from the Israelites' regret noted in Exodus 14?

3. How can you look to God's deliverance of his chosen people to encourage your daily walk?

4. What are ways you have overcome feelings of regret? How can you ask God to help you?

5. How might you encourage a friend who is struggling with regret?

Faith in the Unseen

Because we look not at what can be seen but at what cannot be seen, for what can be seen is temporary, but what cannot be seen is eternal.

—2 CORINTHIANS 4:18

Just because we can't see something doesn't mean it's not there. In the Bible God is recorded to have appeared in several forms—a burning bush, a bright light, a booming voice, a cloud, and, most significantly, in human form through his Son, Jesus. Since Jesus' ascension, we must rely on feeling the presence of God rather than seeing it. The Holy Spirit is our helper and guide.

We live in a society where seeing is the main focus. People are obsessed with videos and photos. I read a recent report that stated people watch an average of 86 minutes of video every day, and five billion photos are taken every day around the world! Five billion photos per day! People are addicted to seeing and documenting things. Everyone wants proof before they commit to an idea or belief. We yearn to see God and have assurance in his directives. I'm confident this isn't just a dilemma of our current time.

Though the Israelites had witnessed the mighty work of God with the plagues in Egypt, though they saw Pharaoh's army swallowed in the Red Sea, the moment they were without a physical reminder of their connection to God and his deliverance through Moses, they turned to creating an idol they could see. They worshiped an object of their own making. Some of us have a hard time picking God over almost anything else we can see. Faith is a daily discipline for us, choosing to follow God's directions for our time rather than what the popular opinion of the day is.

There are two Greek words used in the New Testament that reference time: *chronos* and *kairos*. Chronos refers to the literal passing of time. Kairos denotes the opportune or right time. When I did a lexicon search for both words, I was surprised by what I found: Chronos is used 54 times in the New Testament, while Kairos is used 86 times. The call to us believers is clear—be ready for the opportune time. Be looking for God's guidance daily. When we fill our time (chronos) with things pulling us away from God, we might be turning our eyes from searching for the opportunity to embrace God's offering of time (kairos) that he sets before us. Kairos requires faith in the unseen.

The things that we can see are temporary; they will fade over time. Second Corinthians 4 reminds us that the objects we can hold, see, smell, and taste are not permanent. They offer us temporary promise and provision. And Habakkuk 2:18 says "What use is an idol once its maker has shaped it—a cast image, a teacher of lies?" Man-made objects distract me from giving my devotion to God. The "cast images" I encounter daily are distractions from my attentiveness to experiencing kairos on a regular basis. But I take comfort in knowing God is present beyond my ability to see and he is working in my life even when I can't sense his presence. Only God is eternal. Though we can't see him or the Holy Spirit, we are offered assurance in both chronos and kairos.

Questions

1. How do you have faith in God even though you can't physically see him?

2. How have you seen God at work in your life?

3. How have the things you can see failed you?

4. What are ways you have followed God's directives for your life even when it wasn't the popular belief at the time?

5. When have you had to move forward in faith? What happened?

6. What are some "kairos" moments that have been placed in your path?

Rest in the Present You

Not that I have already obtained this or have already reached the goal,

but I press on to lay hold of that for which Christ has laid hold of me.

Brothers and sisters, I do not consider that I have laid hold of it, but one

thing I have laid hold of: forgetting what lies behind and straining forward

to what lies ahead, I press on toward the goal, toward the prize of the

heavenly call of God in Christ Jesus. Let those of us, then, who are mature

think this way, and if you think differently about anything,

this, too, God will reveal to you.

—Philippians 3:12–15

I do this all the time: I compare myself to a past or future version of myself. I diminish where I am currently because I know there is a better version of me out there if I just look far enough, forward or back. One example of this is when my mind tells me if I'm not in constant motion, I will be left behind or labeled as lazy and unmotivated. When I perceive that I was a better version of myself last year or will be a better version of myself next week, the wrestling game begins. Round and round in my head, stealing the joy of who I am today.

When I start worrying about how I compare to the past or the future me, I am distracted and stop inviting God into the present moment. Any time I view myself through the lens of "less than" and believe its negative lies, I reject the promise of God's plan for my life. By ranking myself in comparison to what could be or what was, I diminish who I am right now. I even stunt my ability to be grateful or grow!

When we read Philippians 3, we see that it's not about being the best version of ourselves, it's about accepting Jesus into where we are right now. When we "forget what lies behind" we give ourselves permission to be present in exactly who we are today in the presence of our Savior. Maybe it's past sins that we can't let go of or negative feelings about ourselves that seem to creep into our present moment. Philippians 3 clearly reminds us to release the pain of the past to fully embrace the present.

And while we might be tempted to read "pressing forward to what lies ahead" as a challenge to seek betterment in the future, the key is to notice what we are pressing toward—the call of God to each of us, not the call of a better self. When we seek to be in Jesus' presence, we're able to silence worry about who we were in the past or who we might be in the future. When we pursue our own selfish "best version" of ourselves allowing that to become more important than being a child of God, we neglect the grace freely given to us in perfect love.

Each day can be an offering, a renewed commitment to be whole and holy, God's beloved child. When we embrace this, we are able to release the sins of the past and settle into God's idea of who we can become. When we accept and practice resting in who we are in Jesus' presence, we are able to fully accept ourselves washed in Jesus' grace. Striving to be a better version is left at the feet of Christ. I dare you: Rest where God has you right now.

Questions

1. What are past mistakes or sins that you can't seem to let go of? Ask God to help you release these.

2. What would you say to a friend who struggles to see themselves as a child of God?

3. What areas of your life can you enjoy right now?

4. How can you rest in who you are today?

A Time For...

A Time for Self-Care

"People do not light a lamp and put it under a bushel basket; rather,
they put it on the lampstand, and it gives light to all in the house."

—MATTHEW 5:15

elf-care has become a bit of a buzz word. It's equated with massages, manicures, a fun vacation, or any number of other "relaxing" ideas. Recent history has deemed self-care as luxurious and something not all of us have access to. Some of us don't feel we have the time for self-care; others of us don't think we have the money for splurging on ourselves. If we allow too narrow of an understanding of what true self-care is, we fall in danger of ignoring our needs and replenishing ourselves to fulfill God's call to be light in the world.

Matthew 5:15 tells us to resist hiding our lights. When we neglect taking care of ourselves, we are on a high-risk path of allowing our lights to dim. God placed us here with thought and intention. The God who knows the number of hairs on each of our heads also knows our needs and our capacity. He placed a light within each of us. Our job is not only to shine but to also steward that light. When we employ self-care, we nourish our light. When we take care of everyone else and leave our needs unmet, we slowly run out of energy.

Proverbs 17:22 says, "A cheerful heart is a good medicine, but a downcast spirit dries up the bones." This is a clear warning that that when we allow our spirit to become crushed, we neglect caring for the person God created us to be. This may not be putting our light under a bushel, but it certainly causes the light to dim with the potential of having the light go out completely.

Some of us have put so many things on the "must do" and "super important" list that we've forgotten to take a breath and care for ourselves. Our minds and our bodies are serving others within our own homes and throughout the community. Some of us have enthusiastically signed up for activities or mindlessly said yes to commitments without really thinking through how it will all get done. Maybe there is work or other social pressure to fill up the calendar or push you beyond your normal routines, and that's okay for a short period of time. But where does self-care discipline kick in and whisper, "Time to recharge"? Have you given yourself permission to decline an engagement, schedule quiet time for yourself, or treat yourself to a simple moment of "me time"?

While contemporary definitions and understandings of self-care sway toward the extravagant spa day, the truth is taking care of yourself is simply assessing your emotional, spiritual, and physical needs each day. Some of the ways I care for myself are listening to worship music, reading a good book, going for a walk or run by myself, and enjoying a weekly Bible study with other women. Self-care doesn't need to be extravagant, and it doesn't have to cost money. Instead, self-care is simply asking God and ourselves how to best care for the light he placed within each of us.

Questions

1. When you hear the word *self-care*, what do you think of?

2. What simple pleasures do you enjoy that don't cost money but help you to recharge?

3. How are you applying self-care in your life each week?

4. If you struggle with self-care, what is holding you back? What one thing might you do to incorporate more life-giving moments into your daily life?

5. How can you encourage self-care with your family and friends?

A Time for Serving

He sat down, called the twelve, and said to them, "
Whoever wants to be first must be last of all and servant of all."

—MARK 9:35

Most of us will say that we want to help others. We see the value in lending a hand when someone is in need. Many corporate workplaces even offer employees time away from the office to volunteer and serve the greater community. Helping is encouraged.

But usually our desire to help comes with other caveats. Things like, "I'll help when it's convenient," or "The opportunity to help must match my interests and skills." Often when the time comes to serve, we don't. We have plenty of reasons that justify our unhelpfulness: "I'm too busy," or "It's not the right time in my schedule."

When we read through the Bible and diligently focus on the topic of serving, we start to realize how unglamorous servanthood appears in Scripture. God seems to be asking his faithful followers to serve whenever it is needed, not when it works for our schedule or our interests.

What does it look like to serve others in the way God asks us to? Surprise! It is a 24/7 job. God isn't inviting us to serve when we want to. He is asking us to serve when the need arises. God is asking that we look beyond ourselves—to see the needs of the people around us. When we allow our own interests and agenda to dictate how we serve, the action of serving becomes more about ourselves and our needs rather than about the person or group in need.

In Philippians 2:4, the apostle Paul states, "Let each of you look not to your own interests but to the interests of others." As God's children we are called to turn away from ourselves and look outward to the people around us. Oftentimes taking a break from self-absorption reveals a multitude of opportunities to serve.

One of Jesus' most memorable messages is found in Mark 9:35: the first must be last. He adds another stipulation—the first must not only be last but must be the servant of all. In this passage Jesus is talking about himself. He steps down from his position of power in order to serve us. He becomes the ultimate role model. He doesn't ask us to do anything he isn't willing to do. He shows up to live out God's call. Serving will not always be convenient.

Serving is a form of sacrifice. It is an offering of our time. There's no perfect time to serve. There's no perfect way to serve. The needs of the world will likely always outweigh the resources. Showing up with a willing heart not only serves the intended recipient but also reminds us it's not about what we can do, it's about what Jesus can do through us. When we look to Jesus as our example of what it means to serve, we need to look no further than the cross.

What does it mean to look beyond your own interests? What might come from asking God, "Whom shall I serve today?"

Questions

1. What acts of service do you intentionally choose each day?

2. How can you look beyond your own interests to see the needs of the people around you?

3. What currently stops you from seeking opportunities to serve? How can you change this?

4. What has been your best experience serving?

5. What skills and passions do you possess that might be useful to those around you?

A Time for Accepting Help

And he answered, "You shall love the Lord your God with all your heart

and with all your soul and with all your strength and with all your mind

and your neighbor as yourself."

—LUKE 10:27

Many of us are not good at asking for help, and we're even worse at accepting it. There's something about getting help that makes us feel inadequate, like we couldn't meet our own needs. We don't want to impose upon others. We're worried about being too needy. Or maybe we're concerned we'll owe someone something we can't repay.

Our resistance to asking for help does not negate our need for it. All of us need help. God created us to be communal people. In Luke 10:27, Jesus instructs us about the importance of neighbors. We are to love our neighbors as we love ourselves. Many times when I've read this passage, I thought it only applied to helping others. But I've come to believe that it also applies to allowing others to help us. When others love their neighbor, it could be they are loving me. I don't need to know all the answers or be self-reliant all the time. And my inability to accept help takes away the opportunity for someone else to love me when I need it. While I might feel like I'm trying to be considerate of other people, my desire to self-protect or turn away assistance can also turn into a fault.

In Ephesians we see that our salvation is not of our own doing. "For by grace you have been saved through faith, and this is not your own doing; it is the gift of God—not the result of works, so that no one may boast" (Ephesians 2:8–9). Just as time is God's gift, so is the work that Jesus did on the cross in wiping away our sin. There is no pride in our salvation. When we resist asking and accepting help from others, we hold onto a prideful heart rather than a humble one.

In accepting the grace given by God, we place ourselves in a vulnerable posture. Our need builds our intimacy with God. Similarly, when we are vulnerable and admit to our needs with the people around us, we foster intimacy. Accepting love from a neighbor opens the door to new ways of loving within community.

Questions

1. How do you feel about asking for help? In what circumstances do you hesitate asking for assistance?

2. How do you feel when you are able to help others?

3. In what ways to you love your neighbor well?

4. How could you improve loving your neighbor?

5. What is one area of life in which you can ask for or accept help this month?

A Time for Health

Or do you not know that your body is a temple of the Holy Spirit within you, which you have from God, and that you are not your own? For you were bought with a price; therefore glorify God in your body.

—1 CORINTHIANS 6:19–20

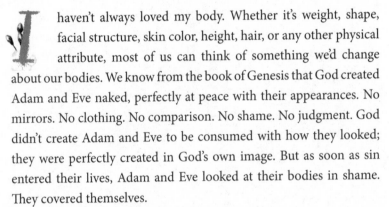

I haven't always loved my body. Whether it's weight, shape, facial structure, skin color, height, hair, or any other physical attribute, most of us can think of something we'd change about our bodies. We know from the book of Genesis that God created Adam and Eve naked, perfectly at peace with their appearances. No mirrors. No clothing. No comparison. No shame. No judgment. God didn't create Adam and Eve to be consumed with how they looked; they were perfectly created in God's own image. But as soon as sin entered their lives, Adam and Eve looked at their bodies in shame. They covered themselves.

Some of us are used to covering our bodies in shame. We restrict our calories to achieve a particular look. We spend countless hours in the gym. We purchase clothing to blend ourselves into our surroundings and look for others' approval. Many turn appearance into its own idol, limiting our relationship with the One who made us.

Health isn't just a number on a scale, a clothing size, or physical strength. Health starts within our hearts. First Corinthians 6 tells us that the human body is a dwelling place for the Holy Spirit. We are commanded to glorify God with our bodies. We should neither deprive them to an extreme nor soothe them to the other extreme. Instead, we should honor God by working toward a loving relationship with the face, arms, hips, hair, and toes God gave us.

Some of us are able to strike a healthy balance easily, but others of us are constantly evaluating what the mirror, scale, or social media tell us in relation to the rest of the world. Continual intimacy with God through prayer, worship, and reading of his Word helps fight off the unhealthy temptations to compare and engage with negative self-talk. Our health—mentally and physically—is important. How we treat our bodies is a reflection of our relationship with God, and we can think of ourselves as stewards of God's temple, a place dedicated to the worship of him.

There is no one-size-fits-all when it comes to how we care for our bodies. And we aren't all meant to have the same shape, color, or physical ability, but we are called to care for our bodies and encourage one another in that process. Take time to nurture your body as a way of honoring your Creator.

Questions

1. What aspects of your body do you really like?

2. What gets in the way of taking care of your body like you want to?

3. In what ways do you take care of your body by making health a priority?

4. How do you think God wants you to improve your health?

5. What automatic negative thoughts do you have about your body?

6. If you begin thinking about your body as a dwelling place for the Holy Spirit, what changes might you make?

A Time for Love

Above all, maintain constant love for one another,

for love covers a multitude of sins.

—1 PETER 4:8

No relationship is perfect. No person will fix whatever we think needs fixing in our lives. It's easy to look toward love and think that all our problems will be solved when we find a solid relationship. While this won't happen, inviting the right person into your heart offers a joy and fullness that is challenging, refining, and rewarding. It's easy, in the chaos of life, to overlook how we interact with those closest to us. Patterns start to form, especially in marriage, that can cause us to take our spouse for granted. While there are different seasons that call for different actions and intentions, we should not use these seasons as an excuse to put love on hold.

There were many times in my life before marriage when I put love on the back burner. Sometimes this was what God was leading me toward; other times I was simply resistant to opening up my heart. Not every season in a single person's life is meant for romance. But there is a time for love. It's easy to want to avoid love, whether you're in a relationship or not. In order to give and receive love, we must be vulnerable. We must give up some control. Most of us know from experience that opening up our hearts and inviting love into our lives doesn't always work out. People get hurt. People get scarred. When a relationship doesn't work out, it can be painful and messy.

Whether you're married or single it's common to idealize what love should look like. In the early stages of a relationship, it's easy to embrace the words of 1 Peter 4:8. We can hold onto the feeling of love for the other person and often overlook many of their shortcomings. But as time goes on, it's harder to allow our love for the other person to flow freely. We start to gripe about their habits or actions. We get worn out and forget the words of 1 Peter. As sinful people, we all need God's grace. And we need grace extended from each other. There is no perfect person, despite what movies or social media depict. As we live in relationship, we must extend a deep love that accepts the imperfections of the one we love just as God has done with each of us.

He calls us to "maintain constant love." If you're married, are you taking your spouse for granted? To foster and grow our relationships, we must put in the time. Not everyone is called to marriage. If you are single, what season are you in? Are you seeking opportunities to love those around you? Are you avoiding love because you refuse to be vulnerable? Take an honest assessment. Whether it's with a spouse, a significant other, or a family member, make time for love.

Questions

1. How do you like to receive love?

2. In what ways do you like to give love?

3. If you are single, how could you show love to those in your life right now?

4. If you are married, what is one action you could do today to show your spouse love?

5. Are there past hurts that hold you back from loving freely? Write out a prayer asking God to help strengthen you in letting go and moving forward in your relationships.

A Time for Listening

DAY
57

Fools think their own way is right, but the wise listen to advice.

—PROVERBS 12:15

I always hated group projects in school. Inevitably someone ended up doing most of the work. People didn't agree. Everyone talked or no one talked. There was a lot of wasted time trying to sort out who would do what. It always felt like a lot of work, which yielded few results. Group projects required that we listen to each other, even when we had differing opinions. Listening is hard. Most of us think we are doing an okay job and listening to those around us, but when it comes down to it, we aren't. Some of us are interrupting in the middle of a sentence. Some of us are thinking about what to say next when the other person stops talking. Most of us are tuning out instead of truly listening.

Proverbs 12 makes it clear that when we stop listening to people around us, we become foolish. If we never allow ourselves to listen, we are missing out. We're missing out on connecting, experiencing how another individual feels and thinks about the world. We are missing out on understanding a different perspective. We could be missing out on accepting wise counsel.

With so many divisions in our culture, sometimes we decide not to listen to people who don't agree with our faith or politics or parenting strategy or other ideas we are passionate about. We shut out the voices of those who we think might disagree. While not all words that you hear from others will be wise advice, if we stop listening, we stop allowing ourselves to discern the difference between good and bad advice. We stop challenging our own ideas and beliefs and can fall prey to foolish behavior.

As I look back, I realize that group projects were not only about the material but more about preparing individuals for the people we'll engage with throughout our lives. When we listen to other people's perspectives, we're choosing to live beyond doing things our way. We're learning patience, persistence, communication, and humility. Some agree on how to do the work. Others have a completely different approach. What matters is learning to work well with others. In doing so, we learn to love our neighbors and truly listen to others.

Questions

1. Think back on a group project. Were you the one doing most of the talking? Were you able to listen well?

2. When are you able to focus and listen well? What distracts you from listening?

3. When was a time when you gained insight by listening to someone you didn't agree with?

4. Think of someone you admire who listens well. What makes you feel heard by them and how can you attempt to be more like this person?

5. Practice active listening this week. Stop thinking about what you will say next and simply hear what the person is saying. Make a mental note of what you discover when you do this.

A Time for Friendship

Two are better than one because they have a good reward for their toil.
For if they fall, one will lift up the other, but woe to one who is alone
and falls and does not have another to help.

—ECCLESIASTES 4:9–10

It can be hard to make friends. I've endured seasons of life when I've felt incredibly lonely. At various times, I've been in a new town or phase of life and needed to make new friends who could relate to my circumstances. There are definitely seasons in life when I've had more time to devote to friendships and other seasons when it's felt hard to get together. Regardless of the season, we are meant to cultivate friendship and mutually beneficial connection in our lives.

Every time I've needed to make new friends, I've felt like it wouldn't happen. I was convinced I wouldn't meet someone who understood me or whom I'd enjoy spending time with. It has felt clunky or even like a one-way street as I've tried to develop friendships. The good news is that's normal. Just like planting seeds, some take root and grow, while others never see the light of day. True intimacy in friendship doesn't happen overnight, it happens with time. Time allows us to grow slowly and genuinely. When we make time to invest in people friendships are fed and strengthened.

In Ecclesiastes 4, we read about the fruit of pursuing friendship. Two are better than one. We know God values relationship! He is a triune God: Father, Son, and Holy Spirit. Even in his existence, he models relationship to us. And just as God desires to be in friendship with us, he also desires for us to be blessed by friendship with others. Through friendship we can live out our faith in service, discipleship, and love. Friendship is holy work.

Not everyone whom we attempt to invest in will become a constant friend. Believe me, I know it's not as simple as that. There's no tried-and-true formula for friendship. But when we show up as our authentic selves, with honesty and a willingness to work past any discomfort of unfamiliarity, often friendships develop.

While I have made many friends through different stages of my life, there have also been friendships that have stood the test of time. To be deeply known over many seasons in your life is of utmost value. Good friends are able to challenge you and counsel you. They are able to walk alongside you in seasons of pain and joy. There is fruit to be harvested from friendship when we allow time to cultivate it.

Questions

1. Who are currently some of your closest friends? How long have you been friends with them?

2. When have you been lonely? What helped end the loneliness?

3. When was a time you noticed someone else who seemed lonely? What did you do?

4. What are some examples of friendship from the Bible that encourage you?

5. How do you make time for friendship?

A Time for Justice

Speak out for those who cannot speak, for the rights of all the destitute.

Speak out; judge righteously; defend the rights of the poor and needy.

—PROVERBS 31:8–9

When I was in graduate school to become a physician assistant, I had to take gross anatomy. That meant cutting open dead people. Each of us was assigned to a group of six students to one cadaver for the duration of the class, which meant there were about fifteen cadavers in the room being worked on by different groups. There were men and women, old and young. There were different skin colors. The first thing we learned was how to remove the skin from each cadaver. Once the skin was gone, all the bodies had lungs, hearts, stomachs. There were no signs of skin tone on the inside. A stark reminder that we are all people, more alike than different.

In many ways, as a white woman I am shielded by the color of my skin. The experience of my life is different from the experience of other humans with differing skin tones. Skin color is one issue amid the many inequalities that exist among us. Refugees, women harassed and underpaid in the workplace, human trafficking—the list goes on. It's tempting, when there are so many injustices happening, to become overwhelmed and simply turn away from what we feel we cannot fix. Don't. We must face the problems. While we can't singlehandedly fix all the injustices of the world, we can use our voices to say they're not okay. We can use our hands and feet as an extension of God's love and grace to work in community.

In seeking justice, we open our hearts to feel the pain of others, to weep with those who weep. In seeking justice, we look beyond our own interests and compassionately pursue the interests of the most vulnerable. Philippians 2:3–4 states, "Do nothing from selfish ambition or empty conceit, but in humility regard others as better than yourselves. Let each of you look not to your own interests but to the interests of others." In seeking justice, we recognize that the world's shortcomings are not someone else's problem, they are our problem.

Justice doesn't happen without us fighting for it. Proverbs 31 tells us to speak for those who cannot speak. We must prayerfully open our mouths, especially if we are in a position of privilege and influence. Change can occur when we remain humble and confident, bringing our voice to the conversation. Let action follow. Be aware and actively combat the destruction of another person's value. Resist letting the shortcomings of equality and care for those in less advantaged positions overwhelm us and keep us inactive. When we turn our eyes and hearts toward justice, we allow God to use us in his perfect time to tend to the needs of others. "When justice is done, it is a joy to the righteous but dismay to evildoers" (Proverbs 21:15).

Questions

1. When have you witnessed or experienced injustice based on race, gender, age, or socioeconomic status? What impact did it have on you?

2. How can you use your voice toward changing inequalities and creating more equitable living situations?

3. What words or phrases stand out to you from Proverbs 31:8-9? What is God asking of you?

4. How do you combat being overwhelmed by the injustices of the world?

5. Think of one person who has made a difference in an area of injustice whom you admire. How can you be more like this person throughout the coming months?

6. Read Psalm 37 and be encouraged by God's ultimate power and justice over the world.

A Time for God

Pray without ceasing.

—1 THESSALONIANS 5:17

I struggle with finding the right amount of time to devote to God. Is ten minutes each morning okay? Or, do I need to set aside ten minutes three times a day? How much time in the Word is enough time? Some days I forget to turn to Scripture at all or find I'm opening up my Bible out of obligation more than a stirring in my soul. Even admitting that to myself makes me cringe. Can you relate?

I think many of us have this same struggle at some point in our faith walk. If we believe God is the Creator of the universe, if we believe he sent his only Son to save us from our sins, why are there seasons when we feel too busy for God? Most of us believe that in our best spiritual life, we should dedicate several minutes every morning to quietly sit and read the Bible, write reflections, and pray, and maybe even participate in a weekly Bible study. In our best spiritual life, if we can maintain consistency we'll feel centered and closer to God.

If we know these disciplines are what's best for our body, mind, and soul, why do we get derailed from making time for God? For me, somewhere along the way I created a set of rules for what it looks like to successfully spend time with God. There must be no distractions. It should be early in the day. I must connect deeply with the words I'm reading. It should last a certain amount of time. In creating guidelines for my time with God, I've inherently created roadblocks to "successfully" spend time with God. If I don't have enough time to fit it all in perfectly, I won't do any of it. I tend to put God on a shelf, only taking him down when it fits into my time the way I want it to. This "best practices" approach is an all-or-nothing, ridiculous spin cycle that eventually leads to days without really going to God in prayer or listening to his Word.

The problem is, even in our best spiritual life when we're doing the daily work, when we're spending time reading his Word and praying, we still may be getting it wrong. We might be reading and praying without thought or open hearts. On days when we avoid time with God because we can't do it the "right" way, we're missing out on letting him speak to us no matter the circumstance. God doesn't want ten minutes of daily enlightenment and prayer. He doesn't want just the quiet hours of the morning. He wants all of it. All of our time, all the time. He wants all of us.

Pray without ceasing. What does that look like? It looks like seeking God in all the moments of our day: quiet, loud, busy, boring, cooking, falling asleep, couch, car, bed, treadmill, closet. To dialogue daily with God. To invite him into our conversations, decisions, and actions. To allow him to soften our hearts at the store, in the shower, while changing a diaper, you name it.

Pursuing time in the Word and time in prayer is important. Limiting God to the perfect quiet time means limiting him to certain parts of our lives. What if we pursued our quiet time despite how complete it would be? What if we saw our devotional time as just one of the many conversations we could have with God? We wouldn't avoid prayer because there wasn't enough time. We wouldn't worry about the perfect Bible passage to motivate or change our heart. We would see each instance for what it was—one of the many moments with him. We might even realize we're praying without ceasing.

Questions

1. If you didn't have to worry about a schedule, what would your ideal time with God look like?

2. What distracts and hinders you from spending time with God?

3. Do you pray without ceasing? What does that look like for you?

4. Reflect on a time when you felt closest to God. What was distinct about that time?

5. What ideas and habits could help you set aside time to be with God and maintain consistency?

Conclusion

hen I wrote this book I had hoped my relationship with time would permanently change. I would be healed of all anxiety, frustration, and fear. I would be more present and productive in my life. That didn't happen, not completely. The thing is, reading (or, in this case, writing) doesn't change you. It's not likely you will finish this book and be transformed or healed of all the habits or routine thoughts you've created in respect to time.

There is a difference between passively knowing something is true and actively knowing something is true. When we are passive in our knowledge, we simply allow what we have learned to sit on a shelf deep in the recess of our minds. Maybe sometimes we will reach toward the shelf to reference what we have learned, but the less we employ action, the harder it will be to reach the knowledge. The shelf will always appear just out of reach. Changing our relationship with time requires active participation. You must do the work to encourage change in your life. I must do the work. We must maintain a discipline of seeking God in all ways.

My desire is that this book is a start to your own personal healing in your relationship with time. While I wrote it to myself first and foremost, I pray that it will speak to you just as deeply and that you'll find comfort in knowing you are not alone in this journey. I pray you see fruitful growth.

Where do we go from here? Recognize that what we do with our time matters. Once we truly understand and embrace the intimacy of our relationship with time, as well as our dependence on time, we begin to see each second, minute, and hour as a gift specifically created for us by God.

Make the most of his gift to you!

About the Author

Meredith Barnes has a colorful professional history including assistant in advertising for the Anaheim Angels, costume designer, orthopedic Physician Assistant, cycle instructor, seamstress, and writer. After receiving a Bachelor of Arts degree in Theology from Loyola Marymount University she went on to earn a Master's Degree in Medical Science from Midwestern University.

She is a mother to three energetic and curious boys. She currently resides in Southern California, where she grew up, but considers herself an honorary Midwesterner. She has spent every summer of her life in a family cottage on the Michigan shoreline, and for ten years she lived in Chicago, where she met her husband, Ben.

Meredith can also be found on Instagram: @MeredithBarnesWriter or on her website: www.MeredithBarnesWriter.com where she is committed to finding faith and beauty in her every day.

About Paraclete Press

PARACLETE PRESS IS THE PUBLISHING ARM
of the Cape Cod Benedictine community, the
Community of Jesus. Presenting a full expression
of Christian belief and practice, we reflect the
ecumenical charism of the Community and its
dedication to sacred music, the fine arts, and the
written word.

SCAN
TO
READ

YOU MAY ALSO BE INTERESTED IN . . .

POEMS AND
DEVOTIONS
FOR TIMES OF
UNCERTAINTY

Love
Holds
You

CHRISTINE
VALTERS
PAINTNER

www.paracletepress.com